T0104464

Mather's Theological Compendium

DENNIS MATHER

WESTBOW°
PRESS
A DIVISION OF THOMAS NELSON
& ZONDERVAN

WestBow Press books may be ordered through booksellers or by contacting:

WestBow Press
A Division of Thomas Nelson & Zondervan
1663 Liberty Drive
Bloomington, IN 47403
www.westbowpress.com
1 (866) 928-1240

ISBN: 978-1-4908-2134-4 (sc)
ISBN: 978-1-4908-2133-7 (hc)
ISBN: 978-1-4908-2135-1 (e)

Library of Congress Control Number: 2014900082

Printed in the United States of America.

WestBow Press rev. date: 03/31/2014

Contents

Preface vii

Part 1 Nine Areas of Study from the Word of God 1
    Chapter 1   The Bible 3
    Chapter 2   Things to Know about God 5
    Chapter 3   Jesus Christ, Our Savior 10
    Chapter 4   Salvation, Sanctification, and Election 13
    Chapter 5   The Holy Spirit 20
    Chapter 6   Anthropology..25
    Chapter 7   Angels 31
    Chapter 8   The Church 35
    Chapter 9   The Doctrine of Last Things....................40

Part 2 Three More Things God Wants You to Know 51
    Chapter 10 Dispensationalism.....................................53
    Chapter 11 The Seven Churches of Revelation,
                  Chapters 2 and 3 64
    Chapter 12 The Individuals, Establishments, and
                  Events of the Tribulation Period..............77

Part 3 About Those Spiritual Gifts 105
    Chapter 13 Introduction 107
    Chapter 14 Three Erroneous Things Associated with
                  Spiritual Gifts 109

Chapter 15 The Cessation Found in 1 Corinthians
13:8–12 112

Chapter 16 The Spiritual Gifts Listed and Defined
with Their Greek Definitions.................. 115

Chapter 17 Additional Information about Spiritual
Gifts 131

Conclusion 135

Preface

This book began on February 23, 1969, when I accepted Jesus Christ into my life as my personal savior. The next night I was put into a Bible study group and over the next few months was "rooted and built up in Him and established in the Faith" (Col. 2:7).[1] This is when I learned the precious and awesome truths He wanted me to learn at that time.

In January 1973, I was led to Faith Baptist Bible College in Ankeny, Iowa, where those truths were formulated into a systematic theology. And it was then that everything I was being taught was a perfect amalgamation of what I learned in the Bible study group.

A few years later, after teaching Bible study groups myself, I started categorizing everything I had written for classes I had taken and those I taught.

Then in a short time I started writing this book from the material I had amassed. It is just lately that I was prompted to send the finished manuscript to West Bow Publishing. This is so that I can commit to faithful people what was given so amply to me, so they can teach others (see 2 Timothy 2:2). I pray that you will enjoy this book as much as I have enjoyed writing it!

---

[1] All biblical quotes are the New King James Version, unless a more modern version is employed to clarify what is being said.

Part 1

∞

Nine Areas of Study
from the Word of God

CHAPTER 1

❦

The Bible

God wrote the Bible because He loves us very much. This means He wants us to know Him and His plans for us, which are always for our benefit. This being the case, it is God's words to us.

It is a very interesting book, not only because its content is inerrant and all sufficient, but also for the way it was created, which was through inspiration.

We study three areas at this time. They are the inspiration of the Bible, the inerrancy of the Bible, and the all-sufficiency of the Bible.

I.   The Bible Is Inspired

The original Greek manuscripts of the Bible were written by the Holy Spirit as He moved upon the hearts of humans (2 Pet. 1:20–21). This is known as inspiration, which also means it was "God breathed" (2 Tim. 3:16a).

However, the writers were not mere pens or puppets of God. Of this, Emery H. Bancroft has said, "[There are] manifestly human elements in the Scriptures and peculiarities of style which distinguish the productions of each writer from those of every other."[1] This is why it can be said God worked in and through the writers of Scripture.

II. The Bible Is Inerrant

Inerrancy means there are no errors or flaws in the original manuscripts of the Bible. Every "jot or distinguishing mark" (Matt. 5:18), as well as every word in the original manuscripts, is what God intended to be there.

God has also preserved the truth of the Bible throughout the ages, so most of our modern translations are still free of errors.[2] They still say what He wants them to say.

III. The Bible Is All Sufficient

The all-sufficiency of the Bible means it deals completely with every subject and matter that pertains to life, godliness, and science. It also means that every "jot and distinguishing mark" (Matt. 5:18), as well as every word in the original manuscripts, is "profitable for doctrine, for reproof, for correction, for instruction in righteousness" (2 Tim. 3:16). It is also why there isn't any reason to have additions to it or subtractions from it (Rev. 22:18–19).

---

[1]   Emery H. Bancroft, *Christian Theology* (Grand Rapids, MI: Zondervan Publishing House, 1975), 27.

[2]   I have included the phrase "most of," because some modern translations have been radically changed by either liberalism or the cults.

CHAPTER 2

∞

Things to Know about God

There are three aspects about God that are essential for us to know. They are the oneness and trinity of God, the nature of God, and the providence of God. The oneness and trinity of God explores the fact that, even though God has three entities, He is one person. The nature of God is a study of each entity of God and the attributes associated with each. The providence of God explores God's will in conjunction with humankind's free will.

I.   The Trinity and Oneness of God

God is a trinity, consisting of God the Father, God the Son, and God the Holy Spirit (Matt. 28:19; 2 Cor. 13:14; 1 Pet. 1:2; 1 Jn. 5:7). However, God is not three persons. He is, rather, one person (Deut. 6:4; Isa. 43:10) with three parts, just as an individual is one person with three parts. We have a body, soul, and spirit, so God has the Father, the Son, and the Holy Spirit.

God as one God with three parts can also be seen when we realize an egg has a shell, a white, and a yoke, but it is one egg; elements have three properties: gasses, liquids, and solids, yet they are the same element; and a family consisting of a father, mother, and child is not three families but one family.

II. The Nature of God

Three things are involved when we study the nature of God. They are His essence attributes, His power attributes, and His love attributes.

Essence attributes involve those intransitive, inherent qualities associated with the name 'I Am' of Exodus 3:13–14 and speak of God the Father.

Power attributes show God's magnitude and sovereignty through Jesus Christ. They have transitive and intransitive qualities to them. They also show Jesus as "the fullness of the Godhead bodily" (Col. 2:9).

The love attributes, however, are completely transitive. They reflect how He reaches out to humankind through the Holy Spirit.

A detailed outline of the attributes follows.

A. The Essence Attributes

1. *Self-existence.* God is absolutely independent of all else other than Himself for the perpetuity of His being (Col. 1:17).
2. *Eternality.* God is without beginning or end (Ps. 90:2; Col. 1:17; Heb. 1:8; Rev. 1:8) and is free from all succession of time. This means He contains in Himself the cause of time.

3. *Spirituality.* God is a spirit, invisible and without material substance, so He cannot be truly represented by material things (Jn. 1:18a; 4:24a; Col. 1:15-17).

4. *Infinence.* God, within His power and sovereignty, is not by any means limited by the universe. This means He is very immense and is, therefore, free from all temporal limitations (Acts 17:24, 25; Eph. 1:21; Col. 1:15b).

5. *Immutability.* God, in His essence, power, and love, is exempt from all change. This would also include the preservation of His Word (Eccl. 3:14,15; Heb. 6:17,18a; Phil. 1:6).

B. The Power Attributes

1. *Omnipotence.* God has unlimited power to do whatever He chooses to do, which is in harmony with His nature and by which He can bring to pass anything He wills that is holy and just (Isa. 40:28; Matt. 19:26b; Phil. 3:21c; Rev. 19:1b).

2. *Omniscience.* God has perfect knowledge of all things that are to be known in the past, present, and future (Ps. 139:3–6; Rom. 11:33–36; Heb. 4:13).

3. *Omnipresence.* God can be present anywhere at any time He chooses (Ps. 139:7–12; Acts 17:27).

4. *Holiness.* God is entirely apart from all evil and all that defiles within Himself and in His relationships toward His creatures (Ps. 119:137). This includes impeccability,

which means that, to Him, sin and error was, is, and will be impossible (Num. 23:19; Heb. 6:18).

5. *Justice.* God is entirely just, and all He does is true and correct (Neh. 9:33). Justice also includes the fact that nonconformity to His laws might bring about suffering in the soul and in the flesh, (Ps. 31:9,10; 119:75; 1 Cor. 5:5).

C. The Love Attributes

1. *Trustworthiness.* God fulfills all the promises His love led Him to make to His people (Rom. 8:38,39; Titus 1:2).
2. *Grace.* God exercises goodness toward the unworthy (Rom. 5:2; 6:14; Eph. 1:7; 2:5).
3. *Mercy.* God's nature leads Him to withhold punishment (Mic. 7:18; Titus 3:5).
4. *Vindication.* God protects His children from their enemies (Ps. 27:1–3, 5–6; 34:7; 53:5).
5. *Loving-kindness.* Everything God does is because of His love for humankind (Isa. 54:10; 63:7; Jn. 16:27a; 1 Jn. 4:7–10).

III. The Providence of God

We have seen that God is all powerful yet loving and condescending. However, He also respects the free will of individuals. This being the case, He does not force Himself on humankind but rather pleads, suggests, and provides an abundance of information for our use.

When God's providence and humankind's desires meet, God's will comes about (Prov. 3:5, 6; Rom. 8:28).

CHAPTER 3

❧

Jesus Christ, Our Savior

Jesus Christ is the second entity of the Trinity and is known as "the Word" (Jn. 1:1). It was He who was chosen to come to earth to be "Emanuel," or, "God with us" (Matt. 1:23; Jn. 13:3), and this was accomplished through a virgin birth.

Jesus Christ came to earth as a baby in a manger at Christmas (Lk. 2:11–16), died on a cross for our sins on Good Friday (Matt. 27:50; Lk. 23:46; 1 Cor. 15:3; Rom. 4:25a), and rose again from the dead for our justification on Easter, (Matt, 28:6a; 1 Cor. 15:4; Rom. 4:25b).

The last two entities effectuate our salvation. By doing this, He bridged the gap that separated us from Himself (Isa. 59:1, 2).

I.   The Miraculous Conception and the Virgin Birth of Jesus Christ

Jesus Christ started His earthly ministry with the miraculous conception by the Holy Spirit within the Virgin Mary (Matt. 1:18). Dr. E. H. Bancroft says,

> God … stoop[ed] down from heaven, and in
> prime accord with the Son as His verbal and

eternal expression, and through the co-ordinate
and covenant operation of the Holy Spirit [took]
hold of a cell or seed of the virgin Mary, creating
a new and distinct human nature which the Son
of God took into union with Himself.[3]

Scripture also indicates Mary, Jesus' mother, was a virgin
when our Lord was born (Matt. 1:25). This is why it can be
said His birth was a virgin birth. However, Mark 6:3 indicates
Mary and Joseph had other children, so she did not remain a
virgin all her life.

II. The Absolute Deity and Absolute Humanity of Jesus Christ

Jesus Christ was God and human in one person. This means He
was, "a unique being with two natures, human and divine, in
one body, and with one personality forever."[4] This also means
He had

a human nature that found its personality only
in union with the Divine nature … and a human
nature whose consciousness and will were
developed only in union with the personality
of the [second part of the Trinity].[5]

---

[3] Bancroft, op. cit., 89.

[4] Ibid.

[5] Ibid.

This being the case, Jesus Christ has two natures that are indissolubly united together, and this is how He can be our advocate. He was tempted in everything, as we are in life, yet He stayed without sin (Heb. 4:15).

III. The Atoning Death of Jesus Christ

Jesus Christ, the perfect "Lamb of God" (Jn. 1:29), came to "lay down His life for the sheep" (Jn. 10:15; 1 Cor. 15:3; Rom. 4:25a). This is also portrayed for us in 1 John 2:2, and again in 4:10, which says He is "the propitiation for our sins." Dr. Bancroft says that "the Scriptures teach that Christ suffered in our [place]."[6] Can anything be more awesome than this?

IV. The Bodily Resurrection of Jesus Christ

After three days, God raised Jesus Christ from the dead (1 Cor. 15:4b, 20), so our justification could be completed (Rom. 4:25b). This is also very awesome! It is, in fact, just as awesome as His dying for our sins.

V. The Ascension of Jesus Christ

In Luke 24:51 and Acts 1:9, Jesus Christ ascended to live at the "right hand of God" (Acts 7:55c; Heb. 10:12). So He is now in heaven as our advocate, interceding for us if we sin (Rom. 8:34; Heb. 7:25; 1 Jn. 2:1).

---

[6] Bancroft, op. cit., 99.

CHAPTER 4

❧

Salvation, Sanctification, and Election

In John 14:6, Jesus Christ said, "I am the way, the truth, and the life. No one comes to the Father except through Me." He is the only way to come to God (Acts 4:10-12).

This chapter is about salvation by accepting Jesus Christ into our lives when He offers salvation to us. This is when we are "born again" (Jn. 3:3) through union with God's Son, Jesus Christ. And after salvation it is about being continually brought to the place of being "conformed to the image" of Jesus Christ (Rom. 8:29).

However, the world believes there are many ways to come to God. This is substantiated by the Scripture that says, "wide is the gate and broad is the way that leads to destruction, and there are many who go in by it" (Matt. 7:13b,c,d). It describes the false doctrine of there being other ways besides Jesus to go to God.

Jesus wants us to have a new life (2 Cor. 5:17; Eph. 2:1–7; Col. 2:13,14) and to appropriate this new life by accepting Him personally as our savior (Jn. 1:12; 3:16; 10:9–11; Col. 1:13,14). This means we will be born again as His children forever (Jn. 3:3, 6–8; 10:28, 29; 1 Pet. 1:23).

We can do nothing to gain this new life on our own. Ephesians 2:8, 9 says, "For by grace you have been saved through faith, and that not of yourselves; it is the gift of God, not of works, lest anyone should boast." So we can do nothing to effectuate or keep our salvation, and it is God who "works in us" (Rom. 7:22; Eph. 3:16,20).

I. Being Born Again through Union with Jesus Christ, God's Provision for Salvation

Being "born again" (Jn. 3:3, 7; 1 Pet. 1:23) is salvation coming to us from God (Jn. 1:13) and means we will be united with Jesus Christ forever (Jn. 3:16; 10:28). This also means, as it says in John 10:28, our new life never ends, because we were given "eternal life." We were not given 'intermittent life,' which does end.

This union with Jesus Christ has many advantages, including fellowship with God (1 Cor. 1:9; Eph. 2:13; Phil. 3:10); forgiveness of sins (Col. 1:14; 1 Jn. 1:9); and having the Holy Spirit dwelling within us (Rom. 8:9–11; 1 Cor. 6:19). It also involves conversion (Matt. 18:3; Acts 3:19), faith (Hab. 2:4; Rom. 5:1; Eph. 2:8; 3:17), repentance (2 Tim. 2:23-25; Rev. 2:5), regeneration (Jn. 15:3; Acts 1:8; Titus 3:5), justification (Rom. 4:25–5:1; 1 Cor. 6:11), and adoption (Rom. 8:15; Gal. 4:5; Eph.1:5).

Conversion is our turning to God (1 Thess. 1:9) and uses faith and repentance to accomplish its purposes. E. H. Bancroft says that "conversion is the human side or aspect of the fundamental spiritual change,"[7] and involves the accepting of Jesus Christ as our personal savior (Jn. 1:12).

Regeneration, on the other hand, is the fundamental spiritual change "as viewed from the divine side."[8] So it is "an immediate act of God effected by the Holy Spirit within the soul."[9] Regeneration uses justification and adoption to accomplish its purposes (Rom. 4:25–5:1) and is totally God's doing (Eph. 2:8).

II. Election

We must accept Jesus Christ into our lives to be saved, because we are in a lost condition and can do nothing to obtain right standing before God (Ps. 14:2, 3; 53:2, 3; Rom. 3:12.23; Eph. 2:8, 9). We need salvation, and God in His loving-kindness has provided that salvation by what He did upon the cross of Calvary (Isa. 53:5; Matt. 20:28; Mk. 10:45; Rom. 4:25a; 5:6; Eph. 2:13–16).

However, God also chooses a person for salvation and draws that individual to Himself (Jer. 31:3; Jn. 6:44, 65; Acts 13:48). This is called election and entails two entities that seemingly oppose each other. These two entities are the sovereignty of God in the universe and the free will of humans wherein they have the free will to choose or reject things that concern them.

---

[7] Bancroft, op. cit., 230.

[8] Ibid.

[9] Ibid., 229.

This has brought about two schools of theology: Arminianism and Calvinism.

Arminianism says that since the fall of humankind has not rendered it impossible for us to exercise our free will, we are free to choose or reject salvation, and this salvation is contingent on acceptance or rejection of Jesus Christ (Jn. 1:12; 3:16).

On the other hand, Calvinism says, "Election is ... the sovereign act of God in grace whereby certain persons are chosen from among man-kind for Himself."[10] Isaiah 64:8; John 6:37a; Acts 13:48; Ephesians 1:4,5; and 1 Peter 1:2 attest to this.

The five tenets of Arminianism are

1. Humankind was created in innocence with a free will.
2. Humankind chose sin and fell.
3. God decided to provide salvation for everyone through the atonement of Jesus Christ.
4. The depravity of humankind has not rendered it impossible to exercise its free will.
5. Salvation is conditioned on humankind's acceptance of Jesus Christ as personal savior.

The five tenets of Calvinism are

1. God created humankind.
2. God permitted the fall of humankind.

---

[10] C. I. Scofield, in the *Scofield Bible*, as quoted by Dr. John L. Patten, "Doctrine of Salvation," *Christian Doctrine* (Ankeny, IA: F.B.B.C. Press, 1973), 4.

3. God decided to provide salvation for all people through the atonement of Jesus Christ.
4. God elected some people to have salvation.
5. God decided to draw these elect persons to Himself by the power of the Holy Spirit.

It is portrayed in the Bible that humankind has lost the ability to freely serve and obey God in a way that is totally in agreement with how God would like it to (Ps. 14:2, 3; Eccl. 7:20; Isa. 53:6a; Rom. 3:23; 3:11,12; 8:7). As a result, we cannot help but choose what our fallen nature dictates (Jn. 8:44a, b), and God must take the initiative in salvation.

In fact, He must even put "a spark of faith" within us (Jn. 6:65; Acts 16:14). This is why it says in Romans 1:17 that it is from His "faith" to our "faith".

However, John 1:12 says that "as many as received Him, to them gave He power to become the sons of God." And this says humankind must also receive the gift being offered and accept Jesus Christ through faith (Jn. 3:16; Rom. 5:2; 10:9, 10) to be saved (Jn. 3:18, 36). It is also why there is much evangelistic effort put forth on the part of Christians to get people to the place where they will accept Jesus Christ as personal savior (Matt. 28:19, 20; Mk. 16:15). So both Arminianism and Calvinism must be reckoned with.

By believing in both of them, a new school of theology is created. It is called Parallel Theology and can be seen in many Scripture verses, including John 1:12 and 6:44; Romans 1:16,

17 and John 15:16; 1 Peter 1:5 and 1 John 4:15; Acts 13:48 and Romans 3:26.

This can also be seen by the illustration of a boy asking a girl for a date. There isn't going to be a date unless he asks her for one, and there isn't going to be a date unless she accepts his offer and goes out with him. It is the same in salvation. There isn't going to be salvation until Jesus draws a person to Himself and asks the individual to accept Him. And there isn't going to be salvation until someone accepts Jesus Christ as his or her personal savior.

III. Sanctification

Sanctification means "the state of being purified, or holiness"[11] and involves separating a Christian from sin. It is also wholly God's doing (Jn. 17:22; 1 Pet. 2:24; Ti. 2:14).

Three areas are included when studying sanctification: past sanctification, which is positional sanctification; present sanctification, which is progressive sanctification; and future sanctification, which is glorification.

A. *Positional Sanctification.* E. H. Bancroft says "that which belonged to [God], set apart for His service, was considered holy"[12] is positional sanctification. It is the same thing as justification and is a declaration of our state of being.

---

[11] James Strong, *The Exhaustive Concordance of the Bible* (New York and Nashville: Abingdon Press), item 38 in the Greek dictionary.

[12] Bancroft, *op. cit.*, 244.

B. *Progressive Sanctification.* H. C. Thiessen says this sanctification is, "purification from moral evil and conformation to the image of Christ."[13] Bancroft says that it is the "cleansing and separating [of] His people and making them different from the world."[14] So progressive sanctification is the work of God in our daily lives, wherein we come to be "conformed to the image of [Jesus Christ]" (Rom. 8:29).

C. *Future Sanctification.* Future sanctification, or glorification, not only includes our being with Christ when we die (2 Cor. 5:6–8; Phil. 1:23) but also includes the fact that we will have resurrected bodies fashioned after Christ's glorious body in the future (Phil. 3:21; 1 Cor. 15:35–54).

---

[13] H. C. Thiessen, *Lectures in Systematic Theology* (Grand Rapids, MI: Wm. Eerdmans, 1949), 378.

[14] Bancroft, op. cit., 244.

CHAPTER 5

∽

The Holy Spirit

The Holy Spirit is the third entity of the Trinity (1 Jn. 5:7) and has every right to be called God (Acts 5:3, 4), even though He is not the central figure of our present dispensation, the Church Age (Jn. 16:3–15; Eph. 1:10; Col. 1:14–20; Rev. 5:6; Jn. 1:12). In view of this, He speaks not of Himself but of the person and work of Jesus Christ (Jn. 16:13-15).

The Holy Spirit called Himself the "Paraclete," which means "one called to help."[15] It is a transliteration of the Greek word *parakletos*.[16] English synonyms include "helper," which is used in the New American Standard Version of the Bible, and "comforter," which is found in the King James Version of the Bible.

There are four areas involved when we study the doctrine of the Holy Spirit. They are the indwelling of the Holy Spirit, the baptism of the Holy Spirit, the fillings of the Holy Spirit, and the spiritual gifts.

---

[15] *The American Heritage Dictionary of the English Language* (New York, NY: American Heritage Publishing Co., Inc., 1969).

[16] Strong, op. cit., item 3875.

I.   The Indwelling of the Holy Spirit

The Holy Spirit is constantly working grace[17] within the lives of born-again Christians, because He dwells within them (Jn. 14:17; 1 Cor. 6:19; Col. 1:27; Rom. 8:9.10; 1 Thess. 2:13; 1 Jn. 4:13).[18] This is why their bodies are called temples of the Holy Spirit in 1 Corinthians 3:16.

According to John, chapter 16, the Holy Spirit does three things as He dwells within us. He guides us into all truth (v. 13), He convicts us of sin (v. 8), and He comforts us during trials (v. 7 and John 14:16). This being the case, we should be very happy He is there.

II. The Baptism of the Holy Spirit

The baptism of the Holy Spirit (Rom. 6:3-5) occurs when we were indwelt by Jesus Christ and placed into the body of Christ to become a member of the Universal Church (1 Cor. 12:13-27; 1 Pet. 2:5, 9, 10). It is not separate from the instant of salvation (Rom. 8:9), which means it is not a second work of grace; it happened when we were saved. It is also when we

---

[17]   The word "grace," as found in such passages as Romans 1:7; 1 Corinthians 1:3; 2 Corinthians 1:2; Galatians 1:3; Ephesians 1:2; Philippians 1:2 and Colossians 1:2, means "graciousness of manner, or act, and its reflection in life," or, in other words "joyfulness" (See Strong, op. cit., item 5485.) This being the case, a Christian will constantly show he or she can do the right thing in a gracious way.

[18]   The Holy Spirit, the Spirit of Christ, and the Spirit of God are all three different ways to describe the third entity of God (Jn. 4:24).

were sealed by the Holy Spirit to become a child of God for eternity (2 Cor. 1:21, 22; Eph. 1:13).

"Baptism" is a transliteration of the Latin word *baptisma,* which in the verb form means "to make fully wet." It also comes from the Greek word *baptizein* which means "to dip."[19] In English it means "immersion", therefore, when we accept Jesus Christ into our hearts, we are fully immersed into a new life in Him (Jn. 17:21-23; Rom. 6:3-5; 2 Cor. 5:17; Col. 3:9,10).

III. The Fillings of the Holy Spirit

Fillings of the Holy Spirit are the many subsequent manifestations of the Holy Spirit that are present in the lives of believers. So it is when they are actually "in the Spirit," which should be most of the time for a Christian.

The term "filling" in this context is derived from Ephesians 5:18, where it says, "be filled with the Holy Spirit." To be filled with the Spirit in Greek means "to be completely full."[20] In other words, it means to be all we are intended to be, and in so doing, we can be used to our fullest potential.

---

[19] American Heritage, *op. cit.*

[20] Strong, op. cit. item 4137.

IV. The Spiritual Gifts

Spiritual gifts, or charisma,[21] are indwelling talents within born-again Christians. They were given to them at the moment of salvation, at the baptism of the Holy Spirit (Rom. 8:9; 12:3; 1 Cor. 12:11-13). This means everyone who is saved has at least one of them (Rom. 12:3; Eph. 4:7); every Christian has some special ability[22] he or she can use for the Lord (1 Cor. 12:11; 1 Pet. 4:10).

Spiritual gifts are unique to the individuals who have them, although someone else could have the same gift. How a certain gift is manifested is particular to that individual, because we are all distinctly different (Rom. 12:6a).

There are three main places where spiritual gifts are found in the New Testament. They are 1 Corinthians 12:8–10, Romans 12:6–8, and Ephesians 4:11. These lists have a total of twenty-one gifts. However, prophecy is listed three times, and they are all the same gift. Teacher is listed twice in these lists, but they are the same gift. This means there are 18 gifts listed in those lists.

---

[21] "Charisma" means "a miraculous faculty, or a free gift" (see Strong, op. cit., item 5486.) and is a derivative of the Greek word *charizomai*, which means "to freely give, or grant" (ibid., item 5483). *Charizomai* is a derivative of the Greek word *charis*, which means "grace" (ibid., item 5485). It was described in footnote 17.

Charis is a derivative of the Greek word *chairo*, meaning "to be cheerful; calmly happy; and well off" (ibid., item 5463). This being the case, Christians should be cheerful and gracious when using their spiritual gifts.

[22] We use the term "special ability" in conjunction with spiritual gifts, because they are in actuality special abilities all Christians have in order for them to either speak or minister (1 Pet. 4:11) to others effectively.

In 1 Corinthians 12:28 and 14:26, there are two spiritual gifts not listed previously in the main lists, so the total goes to twenty gifts in all. We will discuss this in detail in part 3.

None of the 20 spiritual gifts has ceased. We will also see this in detail in part 3, where they are listed and defined in detail.

CHAPTER 6

❦

Anthropology

There are three areas for us to study in anthropology. They are our tripartite being, our Christian walk, and our dual nature that gets us into trouble as Christians.

I.   Our Tripartite Being

People were created as tripartite individuals (1 Thess. 5:23). This means they have three parts: a body, a soul, and a spirit, just as God has three parts: the Father, the Son, and the Holy Spirit. This is one of the ways humankind was created "in the image of God" (Gen. 1:27).

First Corinthians 2:11 says everybody has a spirit (see also 1 Corinthians 6:20 and James 2:26), even though it is dead (Eph. 2:1; Col. 2:13; 1 Pet. 4:6; Matt. 8:22). To illustrate, when a person is alive, the body has life in it and he or she can move around and do things. But when a person is dead, the body has no life in it. The body exists, but it cannot move around and do anything on its own volition. This is the way it is with our spirits before we are saved. We have one, but it is dead and cannot move around or do anything—as far as doing anything right in the sight of God. So it is dead unless God speaks to it through the Holy Spirit (Jn. 16:7–15), who quickens it (Jn. 6:63; Rom. 4:17; 8:11; Eph 2:5).[23]

Every member of humankind was born with the capacity to have a conscience (Rom. 1:18–22), but it must be developed from childhood. And because of this capacity, we are basically moral beings.[24] This means we are responsible for our actions after the age of accountability.[25]

The conscience can, however, be ignored (Rom. 1:28a; Heb. 2:1), be seared as with a hot iron (1 Tim. 4:2), and almost be put to death (Heb. 9:14; Rom 2:5). This is why we must not rely on our fleshly wisdom (2 Cor. 1:12; 1 Cor. 1:20, 21; Ja. 3:13–16). We must, instead, be attuned to wisdom that is from above (Ja. 3:17; Prov. 3:5,6).

A person's soul is different than the spirit and consists of three things: intellect, emotion,[26] and will. Intellect consists of: thought, reasoning, imagination, intuition, memory, order, and

---

[23] See Bancroft, op. cit., 177 where he says, "This 'breath of lives' [(Gen. 2:7)] became the spirit of man, the principle of life within him-for as the Lord tells us, 'It is the spirit that quickeneth' – and by the manner of its introduction we are taught that it was a direct impartation from the Creator. We must, of course, carefully avoid confusing it with the Spirit of God, from Whom the Scriptures plainly distinguish it, and Who is represented as bearing witness with our spirit (Rom. 8:16). But we are told in the Book of Proverbs (20:27), it is the candle of the Lord, capable being lighted by His Spirit…"

[24] For further details on the subject, see Patten, op. cit., 4.

[25] The age of accountability is the time when someone understands the condition of his or her life, and the responsibility for that condition. And they also realize they are accountable for any wrongdoings. It occurs at different times for each person and might never be reached if someone is intellectually impaired to a great degree.

[26] See Galatians 5:19–23 for an array of good and bad emotions.

inspiration. Emotions are our feelings coming to the surface, and the will is our ego.

The fact that humankind has three[27] parts differentiates us from animals in that they only have two parts—the body and soul. I believe the soul in animals is not as highly developed as it is in humans and relies on instinct to a great deal. Plants differ from animals in that they only have one part, the body.

II. Our Christian Walk

The doctrine of the Christian walk is known as peripatology. The term "peripatology" has as its base word *peripateo,* which means "to follow someone as a devoted supporter,"[28] or, in other words, "walking with someone as he teaches you."[29]

Examples of peripatology in the Bible are found in Mark 16:12 and Luke 24:13–32, where two of the disciples walked alongside Jesus on the road to Emmaus. Many of the writings of the apostle Paul mention our Christian walk (Rom. 6:4;

---

[27] See Bancroft, op. cit., 177 where he says while commenting on Genesis 2:7 that the human "became a living soul in the sense that spirit and body were completely merged in this third part…There was a perfect blending of his three natures into one, and the soul as the uniting medium became the cause of his individuality, of his existence as a distinct being. It was also to serve the spirit as a covering, and as a means of using the body; nor does Tertullian seem to have erred when he affirmed that the flesh is the body of the soul, the soul that of the spirit."

[28] Strong, op. cit., item 4043.

[29] To say we are walking with the Lord is figurative, because He is living within us as Christians (Rom. 8:10; Col. 1:27; Gal. 2:20). So He is there all the time, teaching us as He walks along with us (Jn. 16:13–15) making it compatible with the doctrine of the indwelling Holy Spirit.

8:1; Eph. 4:1; 1 Thess. 4:1). The apostle John mentions it in 1 John 1:7.

III. Our Dual Nature as Christians

We are admonished in the Bible to "take heed to" ourselves (1 Tim. 4:16), to see if we are in the place God wants us to be (2 Cor. 13:5), which is walking alongside Him. We do not always do this, however, because our stubborn wills get in the way. This happens because, when we were born again, we were given a new nature (2 Cor. 5:17; Gal. 6:15; Eph. 4:24; 2 Pet. 1:4; Gal. 2:20), but it did not abrogate our old sin nature. We still have it (Rom. 7:15; Gal. 6:8; Eph. 4:22; Col. 3:5–10) and are sometimes enticed to go back and live in it (Ja. 1:13–15; 4:1–4). Chastening from the Lord then comes into a believer's life (Rev. 3:19; Heb. 12:6–11). It is designed so we will live in the Spirit rather than in the "old self" (Rom. 7:25; 8:12, 13; Gal. 5:16-18; 6:8).

There are four methods of chastening that can be readily seen. They are "being out of fellowship with God" that a believer can experience, the "turning over to Satan" of a believer's life, the "giving to us of something we really want but isn't good for us" syndrome, and the "premature death" of a believer.

Being out of fellowship with God is when the Lord temporarily hides his face from us[30] (Ps. 143:7), so that we do

---

[30]   When we become born again, the Holy Spirit comes to live in our spirit. But He can, at times of chastening, hide His face from us (Ezek. 24:25; Ps. 143:7), so we do not have the opportunity for fellowship with Him.

not have the opportunity for fellowship with Him. However, when we have known close fellowship with the Lord and then it is taken away, we tend to do what is necessary to get right with Him (2 Tim. 2:26a; Lk. 15:11-24; 1 Jn. 1:9).

The turning over to Satan of a believer's life is found in 1 Corinthians 5:5[31] and 1 Timothy 1:19,20. It is where we completely lose our testimony for the Lord.[32] This happens because we continue to insist on doing our own thing (Isa. 53:6). But again, when a person has known the blessing of living close to the Lord and then must live to the contrary, the individual tends to do what it takes to get back to where he or she once was (Ps. 137:1; Lk. 15:17–20).

The third method of chastening involves the fact that sometimes we want something so bad and have waited for it so long, that God gives it to us (Ps. 106:12–15). In the end, a person might wonder how he or she could have wanted it at all. This is personified by Israel, when it wanted a king like everybody else around them (1 Sam. 8:4-9). God gave them one, but they consequently endured a lot of bad kings. In the end, however, it became an opportunity for God to

---

[31] First Corinthians 5:5 is usually applied to removing someone from the local church. However, it can also be applied to chastening. Israel was taken from its land, so also we are sometimes taken from a life that is in close fellowship with God.

[32] We do not lose our salvation in times of chastening. We might think we have, and others might think we have, but it is certain that we haven't (Phil. 1:6; Rom. 8:35–39; Eph. 1:12–14; 1 Jn. 4:13). This is because we were sealed by Him at salvation (Eph. 1:13), and He has said He will never leave us (Heb. 13:5).

bring a great blessing for everyone by bringing forth the King of Kings.

The fourth method of chastening is the premature physical death of a believer. It implements the concept found in Acts 5:1–11 and 1 John 5:16. It is only done as a last resort, however, because God is slow to anger (Ps. 103:8; Ezek. 20:15-17; Nah. 1:3).

These methods, except for the last one of course, are designed so we will come to the place where we live in close fellowship with Jesus Christ and not in our old selves (Matt. 6:24; Lk. 16:13). In this way, the dross that creeps into our lives is taken away (Prov. 25:4; Isa. 1:25; 48:10).

CHAPTER 7

∽

Angels

There are essentially three types of "spirit" in existence: God (Jn. 4:24; Acts 17:24, 25), angels (Heb. 1:4-14), and humankind (Gen. 1:27; 2:7; 1 Cor. 2:11). Angels are a separate creation from humankind. This means they do not share the same kind of spirit we do. And the souls of humans do not ever become disembodied spirits, walking around on the earth doing good or evil after they die (Heb. 9:27; 2 Cor. 5:8). This is because, according to the Bible, we will always remain human, and they will always remain angels (Heb. 2:5-9; 1 Cor. 6:3). Also, the human spirit "goes back to God who gave it" (Eccl. 12:7), so we do not remain here on earth after we die.

There are two types of angels: good angels and bad angels. Good angels are ministering spirits for humankind (Heb. 1:14; Ps. 34:7; 91:9–11), and bad angels are bent on doing evil all the time (Eph. 6:12; Jude 6). The latter are those angels who followed Lucifer, or Satan, the once-upon-a-time guardian of the throne of God (Ezek. 28:13-15), who fell and took one-third of the angels with him (Rev. 12:3,4,9).

I. Good Angels

As mentioned previously, good angels are guardian angels sent to minister to humankind. These, I believe, are the angels in general (Lk. 2:13), of which there are millions. Other kinds of good angels are the cherubim (Gen. 3:24; 1 Sam. 4:4; Ezek. 10:1–20; Rev. 4:6), who surround and support the throne of God (2 Ki. 19:15; Ps. 18:10; 80:1; 99:1); the seraphim (Isa. 6:2, 6; Rev. 8:3), who are above the throne of God (Isa. 6:1); and the archangels (1 Thess. 4:16; Jude 9), who herald new events (Lk. 1:11-20, 26–38; 1 Thess. 4:16), protect nations (Dan. 10:5–21; 12:1), and are sent to defeat Satan and his angels in their attempt to thwart the plans of God (Rev. 12:7–9).

II. Bad Angels

Bad angels, or demons, are the one-third of the heavenly host that Satan took with him when he fell (Lk. 10:18; Rev. 12:4). There are two kinds of bad angels, those who are kept in prison (Jude 6; Rev. 9:2–11) and those not kept in prison (Ps. 78:49; Dan 10:13; Matt. 12:43-45; Mk. 1:34; 3:11,12; 5:2-14; 6:7; 9:20; Lk. 10:17-20; Acts 10:38;).

Satan is the leader of all bad angels. Scripture indicates he was once a very beautiful angel (Ezek. 28:12c–15), but this is not the case anymore (Isa. 14:12–15). He and his angels do not have any kind of a facsimile of their old selves, and all of what heaven had to offer was lost to them (Isa. 14:15).

We are not told exactly when Satan's fall took place, but we do know he was on earth to tempt humankind before Adam and Eve fell. So he was here for an undetermined amount of time between Genesis 1:1 and 1:2.[33] This being the case, the creation of humankind and a beautiful home for us proposed a threat to Satan's total control of the earth.

III. The Difference between Humans and Angels

First, angels are different from humankind in that they do not have as free a will as we do. In other words, when they make a decision to do something it cannot be changed. This is illustrated by the fact that when Satan determined to do evil, and when one-third of the angels did the same, it has not changed through the ages. They are still acting in gross rebellion toward the Lord and will always act that way.

Another difference between angels and humans is that good angels can go from one tangible level to another without the means of physical death. It is true they must have permission, or a commission, from the Lord to do so, but they can go from spiritual beings to having a physical body and back again when the need arises (Gen. 18:1, 2, 22; Heb. 13:2). Evil angels,

---

[33] We have not been told in Scripture in so many words when Satan fell, but we can ascertain it was before humans were even created. This is because in Genesis 1:2, the Hebrew word for "darkness" is *choshek,* which means "misery; destruction; death; ignorance; sorrow, and wickedness." It comes from the word *chashak,* which means "withholding light." Hence, it is referring to Satan and his angels, who fell before the world was made ready for humankind. See Strong, op. cit., the Hebrew dictionary, items 2821 and 2822 for these definitions.

however, cannot do this. They can move things around in a very limited fashion (Ex. 7:11, 12), but they cannot do anything with this world's elements without the aid of a very strong medium.[34] But Scripture says if we cavort with mediums we are committing sin (Deut. 18:9–14; Gal. 5:20), so it shouldn't be done under any circumstances.

In James 4:7 we are admonished to "resist the devil, and he will flee from [us]", and Ephesians 6:12 says that we are wrestling with spiritual forces at all times. This is seen in the fact there are "doctrines of demons" prevalent in the world (1 Tim. 4:7; 2 Thess. 2:7), and they show up in our churches sometimes. We will study this in the next chapter.

---

[34] Evil angels cannot do anything to humankind unless permission or an invitation is given to them (Isa. 8:19,20; Ja.4:7).

CHAPTER 8

∽

The Church

I. Introduction

The doctrine of the church is sometimes called ecclesiology. This term comes from the Greek word *ekklesia,*[35] which consists of the word *ek,* meaning "out,"[36] and *kaleo,* meaning "to call or summon."[37] It refers to those people who are being called out of the world and actually means, "a called out assembly of people."

There are three kinds of churches in the world. They are the Universal Church, the local church, and the ecumenical church. Two principal ordinances are usually observed in our local churches: communion and baptism. And there are two principal officers present in our local churches—the leader, or leaders, of the church and the deacons.

---

[35] Strong, op. cit., item 1577.

[36] Ibid., item 1537.

[37] Ibid., item 2564.

II. The Three Churches

A. The Universal Church

The Universal Church[38] (1 Cor. 12:13, 27; Heb. 12:23) has as its members everyone who has been saved from the day of Pentecost (Acts 2:1–4) and everyone who will be saved before the rapture of the church (1 Thess. 4:14–17). This means it includes all those who have died as Christians, all those who are alive as Christians right now, and all those who are going to become Christians before the rapture. It only has saved individuals as its members.

B. The Local Church

A local church[39] (Matt. 18:20; 1 Cor. 5:4; Heb. 10:25) is, "an organization of professing Christians in a given locality that is divinely ordained."[40] The members of the church should be gathered together for the purpose of edification, witness, and worship. Edification involves the ministering to others so as to be a help to them in life, witness is our "being ready to give

---

[38] A capital 'C' is used for the universal church, because it is the Body of Christ.

[39] A small 'c' is used for local churches in our study, because local churches are not the Body of Christ. They are, instead, human-made entities that are allowed by the will of God.

[40] Dr. Harry B. Gray, Systematic Theology instructor, Faith Baptist Bible College, on February 29, 1976.

an answer to every man of the hope that is in us" (1 Pet. 3:15), and worship is giving the Lord the honor due Him.

The main difference between the local church and the Universal Church is the latter has no unsaved people in it, and the local church does. Matthew 13:28–30 says the saved and the unsaved will "grow together," and this speaks of the situation in local churches. The perfect situation would be to have an all-saved church membership, but Galatians 2:4 and Jude 4 say unsaved people will "creep in unawares."

The local church is a facsimile of the Universal Church. This is why it has ordinances to show physically what happens spiritually in the Universal Church. Two ordinances that are most commonly practiced in local churches are baptism and communion.

Baptism (Acts 8:36–38; 9:18) is when a person is immersed in water to portray the death, burial, and resurrection a believer experiences when he or she accepts Jesus Christ as personal savior (Rom. 6:3–5; Matt. 3:4–6). It should only be done by total immersion to properly show that when we were saved our old selves were put to death, old things were buried in the deepest sea, and we were raised to new lives.

Communion is when we corporately remember in our local churches what Jesus did for us on the cross of Calvary (1 Cor. 11:23–26). It is the partaking of unleavened bread and the drinking of nonalcoholic beverages (the fact they should be unleavened and nonalcoholic shows the sinlessness of our Lord Jesus Christ) as a symbol of the brokenness of Jesus' body and the spilling of His blood.

Every local church has a leader, or a plurality of leaders, that can be called by a variety of names. For instance, they can be called pastors, elders, bishops, or even overseers (Eph. 4:11; Titus 1:5; 1 Tim. 5:17; Acts 20:28; Titus 1:7; 1 Tim. 3:1, 2). These names can be used synonymously to describe the same person (Acts 20:17, 28; Titus 1:5–9; Eph. 4:11). These individuals should not only be divinely ordained (Acts 14:23) but should also have leadership gifts of the Holy Spirit. In this way, they will be able to "shepherd the flock of God" effectively (Acts 20:28).

Another officer of the local church is the deacon. The word "deacon" is derived from the Greek term *diakonos*, which means "a waiter."[41] It originally described the purpose of giving church leaders more time for "Bible study and prayer" (Acts 6:1–7).

Qualifications for each of these offices can be found in 1 Timothy, chapter 3.

C. The Ecumenical Church

Another church present in the world today is the ecumenical church. This church says it is the "real thing," (Rev. 17:3-7; 17:18-18:4; 18:20-24) but in actuality, it is only a caricature of the one already in existence, which is the Universal Church.

Ecumenical churches are formed when local churches that have gone apostate[42] consolidate themselves to become an

---

[41] Strong, op. cit., item 1249.

[42] Apostate means "to leave your first estate." So these churches at one time could have been biblical in their beliefs, but they slowly left believing this way.

even stronger false spiritual force. So hence, it is humankind trying to do what God is already doing, which is "building His Church" (Matt. 16:18; 1 Pet. 2:5).

The reason this church is in so much error is that over a long period, bad doctrine tends to be propagated. It is caused by a large concentration of unsaved people among the church membership, and it is really accelerated if the leadership is unsaved. Among the bad doctrines are thinking church membership saves you, baptism saves you, keeping the sacraments saves you, and just thinking being good and doing good works saves a person. Another bad doctrine is calling the local church "the Body of Christ." That term is reserved for the Universal Church (Rom. 12:4,5).

All of the above show that members of the ecumenical church are serving the local church as a means of salvation. But we know it must be belief in Jesus Christ and Him only that constitutes salvation (Jn. 14:6).

III. The Purpose of the Local Church

The purpose of the local church is to be "the pillar and ground of the truth" (1 Tim. 3:15). If this ceases to be, it has lost its mission, and Laodiceanism takes over (Rev. 3:14–19). Let's keep our churches spiritually and doctrinally pure (2 Cor. 7:1), so they will not go from local churches to becoming ecumenical churches.

CHAPTER 9

∞

The Doctrine of Last Things

The doctrine of last things, sometimes called eschatology, is the study of certain events of the last days. It is the Greek words *eschatos* and *ology* put together, eschatos meaning "latter end."[43] It speaks of those things that will happen at the end of, or directly after, our present dispensation.[44]

We do not exactly know when these events will take place, because "it is not for [us] to know" (Acts 1:7). However, we can know the general time frame (Lk. 21:29–31). And one of the best ways of knowing this is the fact that Israel is being regathered, which takes place in the last days (Ezek. 36:24; 37:21; Zeph. 3:14–20; Zech. 10:6–12; Rom. 9:27,28). Israel is getting ready for what God has in store for it, which is having its Messiah sitting on David's throne in Jerusalem (Mic. 4:7; Zech. 10:12), even though the country is now in a state of unbelief. On top of this, the gathering "of all nations against Jerusalem to battle," spoken of in the Bible (Zech. 12:2; 14:2), is beginning as shown by the hatred of many people for the Jewish state, especially those in its immediate vicinity.

---

[43] Strong, op. cit., item 2078.

[44] The seven dispensations will be discussed in the next chapter, which is chapter 10.

We examine seven things in this chapter. They are the apostasy, the rapture, the tribulation period, the glorious second coming of Jesus Christ, the resurrections and judgments, the millennium, and the new heaven and the new earth.

I. The Apostasy

The apostasy is where we are living now. It is based on the fact that "the mystery of lawlessness is already at work" (2 Thess. 2:7), and the stage is being set for those things that are going to happen after our present dispensation ends. So it is good to know what is going on in our present day.

Many things are included in this apostasy. Three of them are humankind is now in a condition that is commensurate with that depicted in 2 Timothy 3:1–7; there is an increase of knowledge that comes about predicted by Daniel in Daniel 12:4; and the world can only think of one thing, and that is the quest to become a one-world society. So it can also be seen by these facts that we are in the last days just prior to the rapture (Matt. 24:32, 33, 37; 2 Thess. 2:7, 8; Ja. 5:9; 1 Jn. 4:17b).

II. The Rapture

The rapture is when born-again Christians of all nations will be delivered from "the wrath to come" (1 Thess. 1:10; Rev. 3:10). It is the event that will end the church dispensation and the next event in eschatological history.

In the rapture we will be brought up into the clouds to be with Jesus Christ (1 Thess. 4:14–18), and it is certainly our "blessed hope" (Titus 2:13). It is also why everyone who is born again is at the "marriage" and the "marriage supper" of the Lamb in heaven (2 Cor. 5:8; Rev. 19:7, 9), while everyone who does not participate in it is left on earth to go through the tribulation.

III. The Tribulation

The tribulation is that period between the rapture and the glorious second coming of Jesus Christ. It takes place on earth, while born-again believers are in heaven.[45] It has also been known as Daniel's seventieth week (Dan. 9:24–27),[46] the time of "Jacob's trouble" (Jer. 30:4–9), and the "hour of trial" for the gentiles (Rev. 3:10).

The tribulation period is seven years in length and has two halves (Dan. 9:27), each three and one-half years long. The first half sees the regimes of the Antichrist and the False

---

[45] We are in heaven only for a short time, because Revelation 19:14 says we will be coming back with Jesus when He returns. We go to heaven to sleep right now when we die (Mk. 5:39; 1 Cor. 15:51; 1 Thess. 4:14, 15; Song 5:2), and when we awake, we are to have a great banquet (Rev. 19:7–9).

[46] Daniel's seventieth week is based on the fact the weeks in Daniel chapter 9 are seven-year periods. It also includes the fact that the church dispensation is a parenthesis inside the kingship dispensation between the sixty-ninth and seventieth weeks. This is so the gentiles can come to know the Messiah and is portrayed for us in Romans 9:24–30 and 11:1-17.

Prophet come into being.⁴⁷ Only during this time will the world see these two in power (2 Thess. 2:7, 8).

Israel has somewhat peaceful conditions in the first half of the tribulation, because it has entered into a peace pact with the Antichrist (Dan. 9:27; 11:21–23; Isa. 28:14–18) through the help of the False Prophet (Zech. 11:16, 17; Rev. 13:12; Rev. 18:3). But even this treaty does not ensure a lasting peace for Israel, because at the halfway mark of the tribulation, the Antichrist and the False Prophet desecrate the temple that has been built in Jerusalem (Dan. 11:31; Matt. 24:15). This is when half of the people of Israel flee to a safe place (Zech. 14:2; Matt. 24:16–20; Mk. 13:14–20; Lk. 21:20, 21; Rev. 12:6, 14–16) that has been prepared for it in the countries of Edom, Moab, and Ammon (Dan. 11:41; Rev. 12:16a).⁴⁸

The second half of the tribulation is when our Lord judges the earth. Much is said in the Bible about this (Zech. 14:1–6; Rev. 6:12–17; 8:7–13; 9:1-21; 14:18–20; 16:1–21; 19:17–21), because God does not wish for anybody to go through it (2 Pet.

---

⁴⁷ The Antichrist will someday be the dictator of the world (Rev. 13:1–10; Dan. 11:21–45; Rev. 17:7, 8, 11), and the False Prophet will someday be the leader of the "one-world church" (Rev. 13:11–18; 17:1b–6, 9, 18; 18:2–24).

⁴⁸ In *The Wycliffe Bible Commentary* (Nashville, TN: The Southwestern Co., 1962), Wilbur Smith says while commenting on Revelation 12:13–17 that "the earth's aiding the woman (v. 16) may represent, as Walter Scott says, the governments of the earth befriending the Jew 'and providentially (how, we know not) frustrating the efforts of the serpent.'" So the countries south and east of Israel, where Saudi Arabia is now located (Edom, Moab, and Ammon are ancient Arabic countries that were in the general area that is now the country of Saudi Arabia), will again aid Israel in the future, when she is under persecution. They did this unknowingly in 1991, during the Persian Gulf War, when it was thought the leader of Iraq, Saddam Hussein, had as one of his goals the destruction of Israel.

3:9). The first half of the tribulation may bring wars, famines, diseases, and a dictator (Rev. 6:1–9), but the second half brings cataclysmic devastation as no one has ever seen (Rev. 6:12–17). That this period is very short is indicative of the fact God is very merciful (Matt. 24:22; Mk. 13:19, 20).

IV. The Glorious Return of Jesus Christ

Jesus Christ will be coming back, once to take His children away (known as the rapture), before the great tribulation period (1 Thess. 4:14–18), and a second time to stay at least one thousand years as "King of Kings and Lord of Lords" (Rev. 17:14; 19:16). The latter time is known as the glorious return of Jesus Christ. (Rev. 19:11), and is when He establishes His millennial kingdom on earth to reign as the Prince of Peace (Rev. 19:11–16; 20:4– 6; Isa. 11:6-11; Ezek. 34:11-15; Amos 9:11–15; Mic. 4:1-13; Zeph. 3:9–20; Zech. 8:3–8, 11-23; 13:9–14:21).

The glorious return of Jesus Christ is also known as the second coming of Jesus Christ, because it is the second time He actually puts His feet on the ground.[49] It occurs at the end of the tribulation period and is for the purpose of curtailing the activities of both the Antichrist and the False Prophet. Jesus comes quickly, as He said He would (Rev. 3:11; 22:7, 12, 20), and the Antichrist and the False Prophet are put

---

[49] At the rapture, Jesus catches us up into the clouds (1 Thess. 4:17), but at the second coming, He comes down through the clouds and puts His feet on the ground (Isa. 12:6c; Dan. 7:14). It is putting His feet on the ground that constitutes an advent.

directly into "the lake of fire burning with brimstone" (Rev. 19:20). Everyone else present at this pseudo-battle known as Armageddon is slain "with the sword which proceeded from the mouth of Him who sat on the horse" (Rev. 19:21). And this person sitting on the horse is Jesus Christ at His second coming.

V. The Resurrections and Judgments

There are three resurrections in the future that are in conjunction with three judgments. They are one that pertains to born-again Christians, one that pertains to righteous Old Testament saints, and one that is for the unsaved of all ages.

A. The Resurrection and Judgment for Christians

The resurrection we are speaking of for Christians is the rapture (1 Thess. 4:17), and the judgment is the judgment seat of Christ (2 Cor. 5:10). The judgment seat of Christ is also called "the bema seat," the place where the Greek participants of the Olympics went to get their rewards. So also we go to this judgment not to receive condemnation (Rom. 8:1) but to receive our rewards for a job that is well done (Matt. 25:21). This does include, however, the fact we might experience the loss of rewards we could have had if we lived a life more in accordance with God's will for us (1 Cor. 3:9–15; 1 Pet. 1:13–19; Rom. 14:10–13).

B. The Resurrection and Judgment for Righteous Old Testament Saints

There is a judgment in conjunction with the resurrection that is found in Daniel 12:1c. It is also not for the purpose of condemnation, because these are saved people. This judgment is for the purpose of giving rewards to everyone who died righteously from the first through fifth dispensations. This is so they will be ready for the millennium.

In addition, this resurrection and judgment are for those who will be saved during the tribulation period.[50] This is why it takes place after the tribulation and before the millennium starts.

C. The Resurrection and Judgment for the Unsaved of All Ages

The judgment the unsaved of all ages encounter is called the "great white throne judgment" (Rev. 20:11–13). It is also known as the "second death" (Rev. 20:5, 6, 14) and is when everybody who has not accepted Jesus Christ as their personal savior throughout all the dispensations are put into the "lake of

---

[50] Many scholars believe that Ephesians 4:8–10 is speaking of when Jesus Christ went to "Abraham's bosom" (Lk. 16:22) and brought its inhabitants to heaven to be with Him. I believe this is true, which is why I believe these people will be at this judgment.

As has been noted, those individuals who are saved during the tribulation period will also be at this judgment. They are the 144,000 Israelites and their converts who are sealed by the Lord in Revelation 7:3–8, the gentiles mentioned in Revelation 7:9–14, and a remnant of Israelites who are found in Revelation 12:6; Zechariah 14:2, 5; and Ezekiel 14:21–23.

fire" for eternity (Rev. 20:14, 15; 22:11).[51] It takes place after the millennium and before the new heaven and new earth are created.

VI. The Millennium

The millennium (Psa. 72:7–17; Isa. 2:2–4; 24:23; 35:1–10; 65:19–25; Jer. 23:5–8; Mic. 4:1–8; Zech. 14:16–19; Rev. 20:3–10) is the one thousand year period after the great tribulation ends and before the new heaven and new earth are created. It is when Jesus Christ reigns in person on King David's throne in Jerusalem (2 Sam. 7:4–17; 1 Chron. 17:4–15; Ps. 2:6; 89:3, 4; Lk. 1:68-75; 2:14, 32; Rev. 19:15) with born-again Christians at His side on the thrones He promised them (1 Cor. 6:2; Rev. 5:10; 20:4).[52]

Everyone who will be saved during the tribulation, as well as those who will be present at the Daniel 12:1–3 resurrection, will go into the millennium to start the nations once again. Jewish people, of course, start the nation of Israel (Ezek. 34:11–31), and gentiles start the other nations (Isa. 2:2,3; Rev. 7:9-17; 20:8).

---

[51] Luke 16:23, 24 indicates people who are in Hades have some sort of a body, so they will be able to stand judgment.

[52] Second Corinthians 5:8 and 1st Thessalonians 4:17 say that either after death or after the rapture, Christians are in the Lord's presence (see footnote 45), and this includes when we reign with Him (Rev. 5:10). I think this includes being in a "palace" on earth during the millennium (Psa. 45:10-15; Song 1:4c).

There is only a partial lifting of the Genesis curse during the millennium, because death is still present (Isa. 65:20), and chastening is still necessary (Jer. 23:5). This is why I believe people who are living on earth during the millennium do so in a resurrected body like Jesus' resurrected body (Jn. 20:17).

However, the resurrected body is not the final one everyone will inhabit. As told in 1 John 3:2, at the creation of the new heaven and earth, everyone who has not perished in judgment will inherit a perfect body called a "spiritual body" (1 Cor. 15:44; Rev. 1:14,15).

There is an apostasy at the end of the millennium, when Satan is released for a little while (Rev. 20:7–10). It is for the purpose of testing those individuals who have been born during the millennium but only have a nominal profession and allegiance to our Lord. In other words, they have not been born again to a heart belief in Jesus Christ. He has given them the chance to live for Him, but in their hearts, they have not really accepted him as Lord (Matt. 7:21).

Needless to say, fire comes down from heaven and devours all those who participate in this rebellion (Rev. 20:9). So these individuals will be found at the great white throne judgment.

VII. The Final State

The final state of the universe is called 'eternity future' because it is beyond the salvation dispensations we are living in right now. It is after a new heaven and a new earth are created (Rev. 21:1), and is when all the curses, including the curse of death, are finally and for all time done away with (Rev. 21:4; 23–27; 22:1-3). It comes after the millennium is completed and after our present heaven and earth are destroyed (2 Pet. 3:10–12). It will also be the way things are going to be for eternity (Rev. 22:11).

Part 2

∞

Three More Things God Wants You to Know

CHAPTER 10

∞

Dispensationalism

I. Introduction

Dispensationalism is when you "rightly [divide] the word of Truth" (2 Tim. 2:15) into dispensations. It is a viable method of biblical interpretation.

But we must define a dispensation. A dispensation, according to the dictionary, is "a dispensing," or "something dispensed."[1] And dispensing on the part of God is when He reaches out and brings fallen humankind back into fellowship with Himself (Lk. 19:10). Bringing fallen humankind into fellowship with Himself is called grace, and God loves to do this. Because of this He has never left the world without a means for accomplishing it (1 Tim. 2:4).

A dispensation is also an administration system. Administration comes from the Latin term *ministrare,* which means "to serve" or "to give out."[2] What is being administered is the grace of God in the form of a salvation plan, and this salvation plan is different for each dispensation (Rom. 11:6; Heb. 10:1, 9). This is because progressive revelation comes

---

[1] Victoria Neufeldt and Andrew N. Sparks, *Webster's New World Dictionary* (New York, NY: Pocket Star Books, 1995).

[2] Ibid. (See the word "administer" for this definition).

into play, and the next dispensation is different from the last (Isa. 28:9, 10).

But in addition to this, a dispensation happens during a time period to ensure everyone who is to be saved is given salvation. This being the case, and to sum it up, a dispensation would be 'an administration of God's grace given for the purpose of bringing humankind back into fellowship with Himself, involving a salvation plan and happening during a period of time'.

II. The Seven Salvation Dispensations

There are seven dispensations during all of salvation history. Six of them have been put into effect so far. They are conscience, human government, patriarch, Mosaic, kingship, and the church. The millennium, which is number seven, is in the future.

The seven dispensations are based on the covenants Scofield lists in the *Scofield Reference Bible*. He lists eight of them, because he lists the Edenic covenant, which is not associated with a salvation dispensation. It is an era of innocence occurring before the fall, just as the period after the millennium called the new heaven and new earth is an era of confirmed righteousness.[3]

The covenants he lists are Edenic (Gen. 2:15–17), Adamic (Gen. 3:15–19; 4:1, 26), Noahic (Gen. 9:6, 13–16; 8:21, 22), Abrahamic (Gen. 12:2), Mosaic (Ex. 19:5), Palestinian (Deut.

---

[3] The Edenic covenant is a dispensation of a sort, but it is not a salvation dispensation. This is because it was in existence before humankind fell in Genesis 3:1–7. It is a pre-salvation era, just as there will be a post-salvation era known as 'eternity future' after the new heaven and new earth are created (Rev. 21:1).

30:1-10), Davidic (2 Sam. 7:16), and the new covenant (Jer. 31:31; Rom. 11:26, 27; Heb. 8:8-13; 12:24a; 13;20). The dispensations are seen to be as follows.

A. *Conscience.* The period immediately after the fall of man to the great flood (Gen. 3:7–7:1). It is portrayed by the Adamic covenant (Gen. 3:16-23).

B. *Human Government.* The time from after the great flood to the Tower of Babel. It is found in Genesis 8:15 to 10:25b and is portrayed by the Noahic covenant (Gen. 8:20–9:6).

C. *Patriarch.* That period from when Abram was called out of Ur to when the Ten Commandments were given at Mt. Sinai (Gen. 12:1–Ex. 19:4). It is portrayed by the Abrahamic covenant (Gen. 12:1–3; 48:3, 4).

D. *Mosaic.* The time between the giving of the Ten Commandments to when the nation of Israel received a king to lead them (Ex. 19:5–2 Sam. 7:7). It is portrayed by the Mosaic covenant (Ex. 20:1–31:18).

E. *Kingship.* The time between the giving of an earthly king for Israel to the day of Pentecost (2 Sam. 7:8–Acts 2:1–4). It is portrayed by the Davidic covenant (2 Sam. 7:4–17).

F. *Church.* That period from the day of Pentecost to the rapture of the church (Acts 2:1–4–Rev. 4:1). It is not portrayed by a

Scofield covenant but by the "everlasting covenant" (Heb. 12:24a; 13:20), of which Unger says it is, "the covenant of unconditional blessing based upon the finished redemption of Christ."[4] And one of the blessings involved during the church dispensation is the fact that we, as born-again Christians, are not going to face the hardship of having to go through the great tribulation.[5]

Another blessing is that we share in the new covenant. This is seen in Romans 11:11-18 and means that we share 'the Kingdom of God' with Israel (Heb. 12:22-24).

G. *Millennium.* The period after the glorious second coming of Jesus Christ (Rev. 19:11–21), at the end of the tribulation, to when the one thousand years are over (Rev. 20:1–6; Zech. 14:8–11; Joel 3:16–18; Isa. 35:7–10). It is in fulfillment of the Davidic, the Palestinian, and the new covenants (Jer. 31:31–33; Rom. 11:25- 27; Heb. 8:8-13).

---

[4] Merrill F. Unger, *Unger's Bible Handbook* (Chicago, IL: Moody Press, 1967), 766.

[5] The great tribulation (Rev. 6:1–19:21) is a parenthesis in dispensational history for the purpose of judgment, much the same as the great flood of Noah's day (Gen. 7:1–24) and the great disbursement at the time of the Tower of Babel (Gen. 11:1–9). However, after the rapture happens, the kingship dispensation resumes, making the church dispensation an actual parenthesis within the kingship dispensation. See Daniel 9:24–27 for an explanation of this.

Israel, since they collectively as a nation did not accept Jesus Christ as their Messiah before the church dispensation (and if they would have done this, they would have had the privilege of experiencing the millennium before the church dispensation), will also go through the judgment of the great tribulation. However, when things get really bad, they do experience God's protection by being hidden out in the wilderness (Rev. 12:14–16).

III. Progressive Revelation and Progressive Illumination

The dispensations involve a very important concept called progressive revelation. Each dispensation starts with the revealing of new truths that build on the information that has already been revealed. This makes it easier to understand God's plan for redemption.

However, there is also a concept called progressive illumination. This occurs when those truths that have already been revealed to humankind are individually taught to each person (Jn. 14:17; 16:13–15, 25; 2 Cor. 3:8). It is like this in our colleges and universities. We must take prerequisite courses before we can take ones that are advanced. Babies also learn this way. They first learn the sound of your voice, then the features of your face, and finally, they learn your personality.

Each dispensation brings with it a new and better salvation plan, because something new has been revealed. So we must believe there is a difference between each dispensation. What was the salvation plan in one dispensation is not the salvation plan in another.

For instance, if you believe everyone who is good and keeps the Ten Commandments will be saved on those merits, then you are in error, because that is the way things were done in previous dispensations. It is true that keeping the Ten Commandments is an admirable thing to do, but it is not enough for salvation in our present dispensation. It is instead faith in the Lord Jesus Christ that effectuates salvation in our present day (Acts 4:12; Col. 1:20; 1 Pet. 1:18–20; Ja. 2:10; 2

Cor. 3:6; 15–17; Eph. 2:8, 9; Rom. 4:4, 5; 11:6; 3:27, 28; Gal. 2:16–3:26; Heb. 10:1–9).

IV. The Economies of Each Dispensation

Each dispensation also has an economy. *Webster's Dictionary* says that an economy is "an orderly management or arrangement of parts."[6] So a dispensation involves an administrative management, or in other words, an accountable responsibility. However, it is a responsibility that comes from God and is given to humankind as a stewardship. The following are the economies of each dispensation.

A. In the Conscience Dispensation

The conscience dispensation is where humankind was given the economy to live according to their consciences (Gen. 4:7). When Romans 1:20d says that humankind is "without excuse," because their consciences should tell them there is a God, how much more should the conscience of those who lived immediately after the fall of man be programmed toward the things of God? But it wasn't, because the first murder occurred shortly after the fall (Gen. 4:8)! Remember, during this time the world became very wicked, and violence filled it, (Gen. 6:11).

---

[6] *Webster's New Twentieth Century Dictionary of the English Language* (Cleveland, OH: World Pub. Co., 1960).

B. In the Human Government Dispensation

Each dispensation brings failure on the part of humankind to live up to the stewardship given to it. So a new economy was necessary after the great flood, because humankind failed so miserably during the conscience dispensation.

The economy of this new dispensation was to obey the government that was established for the purpose of governing humankind's heart. It is also when capital punishment was instituted for the purpose of punishing those who killed another human being (Gen. 9:6).

But it seems that another failure became a reality, when humankind decided to change small government to a huge consolidation of all of humankind in the land of Shinar (Gen. 11:2). In Genesis 9:1 God said to, "be fruitful and multiply, and fill the earth." But they didn't fill the earth, and instead decided to build the Tower of Babel (Gen. 11:1-4).

Because of this, another dispensation was necessary.

C. In the Patriarch Dispensation

In the patriarch dispensation God picked Abraham to establish a new nation for Himself (Gen 12:1-3). And it was Abraham's faith in the promise of a great nation (Gen. 15:5,6) that constituted the economy of this dispensation.

A great nation was started, it is true, but it was an ungrateful nation because of certain events in the wilderness (Ex. 15:22–17:7). Because of this, another dispensation became necessary.

D. In the Mosaic Dispensation

In the Mosaic dispensation, laws were given through Moses to the nation of Israel establishing a theocracy (Deut. 5:1-21; 10:12,13;12:1-26:13). These laws involved a major law that was general, or the Ten Commandments, and a secondary law that was specific in its application, which is found in the books of Deuteronomy and Leviticus. This, then, established the obeying of laws in order to be right with God.

But being right with God also involves faith. And this faith, as it has always been, is more than just mere obedience to laws (Heb. 8:6–10). There must also be a love for God, even though it was anti-thematically dependent on keeping the law in this dispensation. But the human heart cannot keep God's laws perfectly, and the responsibility shifted to a king to lead the nation as a whole.

E. In the Kingship Dispensation

During the kingship dispensation, it was the king's responsibility to lead the nation of Israel in God's way (1 Sam. 13:13,14). This was the economy of the kingship dispensation.

But this dispensation was also when a system of sacrificing animals, which was for the purpose of looking forward to a messiah, was in place. But the blood of bulls and goats cannot save you (Heb. 9:8, 9), and another dispensation was necessary.

F. In the Church Dispensation

At the beginning of the church dispensation the day of Pentecost gave us the Holy Spirit to help us live the Christian life. The resurrection and ascension of Jesus Christ had taken place, and the Son of God had come to "take away the sin of the world" (Jn. 1:29; 1 Pet. 2:24; Isa. 53:2–5).

And this is the economy of the church dispensation: it is when all people are to accept Jesus Christ into their hearts as their personal savior (Psa. 2:12; Jn. 1:12) and tell of the "good news of Jesus Christ" (Matt. 28:19, 20; Mk. 16:15).

But now near the end of the church dispensation the true Christianity is in the minority, so a new dispensation is necessary.

G. In the Millennium

The millennium will once again involve Israel in a theocracy. But this time, it is Jesus Christ who is their king. So it is to serve Him as "King of Kings and Lord of Lords" (Rev. 11:15; 20:4) that will be the economy of this dispensation.

V. The Progressive Revelation of the Blood Sacrifice

It was revealed early in Genesis that blood sacrifice was necessary for the appeasement of sin. It was necessary for Adam and Eve when it came time to "clothe" them (Gen. 3:21), and it was necessary when Cain and Abel were to bring sacrifices to God (Gen. 4:1–5). This is because, "without the shedding of blood there is no remission [of sin]" (Heb. 9:22).

We have seen that blood sacrifice was also necessary during the Jewish dispensations. However, the church dispensation is the first dispensation where progressive revelation pointed directly to the Son of God, Jesus Christ, as the ultimate blood sacrifice (Eph. 1:7

So the progressive revelation of the blood sacrifice of Jesus Christ came all the way from Genesis 3:15, where the promise of His first advent was given, on to Genesis 3:21, where blood was shed to atone for sin. Then it went on through the sacrificial systems of the Jewish dispensations to the death of Jesus Christ, who it has been revealed, is "the Lamb of God" (Jn. 1:29, 36). So the blood sacrifice is actually nondispensational and transcends the dispensations.

VI. Jesus Christ as the Object of Faith in All Dispensations

Jesus Christ has been the real object of faith in all dispensations. But before the first advent, much of humankind did not know that it was he who was to come to save them. It was revealed somewhat in the kingship dispensation, because Isaiah 53:2–12 speaks of a person suffering for us; it does not mention Jesus Christ specifically. It is the same in Psalm 2, verses 11 and 12, and this is the most direct reference to the Messiah.

However, the Ethiopian eunuch of Acts, chapter 8, did not know, as he was reading in Isaiah, chapter 53, that it was Jesus Christ he was reading about, and is why Stephen had to go and explain the scripture to him (Acts 8:26-35). Progressive revelation hadn't progressed to the extent that the eunuch knew it was Jesus who was being mentioned. His progressive illumination also hadn't come to that point.

Passages that mention Jesus Christ are scattered throughout the Old Testament. They are in Isaiah 7:14; Micah 5:2; Hosea 11:1; Isaiah 4:2; Jeremiah 23:5; 33:15; Psalm 2:7; Isaiah 42:1–4; 9:2; Psalm 109:1; Isaiah 62:11; Zechariah 9:9; and Psalm 118:22, 23, 26; 22:1–31.

When the first advent came about at the appointed time (Gal. 4:4; Eph. 1:10), the world was ready for Him, because people were looking forward to the coming of the Messiah (Ps. 2:11, 12), just as right now we are looking forward to His return. So it has always been faith in Jesus Christ that is the main focus of revealed truth.

CHAPTER 11

∞

The Seven Churches of Revelation, Chapters 2 and 3

I. Introduction

There are seven churches mentioned in the book of Revelation, chapters 2 and 3, that were in cities that either have been or are still in existence in present-day Turkey. They are Ephesus, Smyrna, Pergamos, Thyatira, Sardis, Philadelphia, and Laodicea.

As we shall see, these churches hold many implications important to us as Christians today. This is because they are indicative of seven church eras that can be seen within the church dispensation, as well as individual church personality types that can be seen among the many churches that are among us today.

II. The Significance of the Seven Churches as They Relate to Church History

Both H. A. Ironside and Henrietta C. Mears have commentaries about each of these churches. I have also elected to compare these passages with a history book I used as the text for a Western history class in college. It is by Stewart C. Easton.

Their definitions, as well as the Scripture references, are used in the following:

A. Ephesus

The first church era is Ephesus. It is found in Revelation 2:1–7.

> To the angel of the church of Ephesus write: "These things says He who holds the seven stars in His right hand, who walks in the midst of the seven golden lampstands:
> "I know your works, your labor, your patience, and that you cannot bear those who are evil. And you have tested those who say they are apostles and are not, and have found them liars; and you have persevered and have patience, and have labored for My name's sake and have not become weary. Nevertheless I have this against you, that you have left your first love …"

H. A. Ironside says in his book *Lectures on the Book of Revelation* that, "Ephesus means 'desirable', such a term as a Greek applied to the maiden of his choice."[7] Henrietta C. Mears says somewhat the same in her book *What the Bible Is All About,* when she says, "Ephesus [is] the church of the first-love,

---

[7]   H. A. Ironside, *Lectures on the Book of Revelation* (Neptune, NJ: Loizeaux Bros., 1969), 37.

the apostolic church."[8] This church would be, then, the book of Acts in the New Testament, where the apostles established new churches. So this church era was truly the age of the first love, from about AD 30 to AD 150.

B. Smyrna

The second church era is Symrna. It is found in Revelation 2:8–11.

> And to the angel of the church in Smyrna write, "these things says the First and the Last, who was dead and came to life: I know your works, tribulation, and poverty (but you are rich); and I know the blasphemy of those who say they are Jews and are not, but are a synagogue of Satan. Do not fear any of those things which you are about to suffer. Indeed, the devil is about to throw some of you in prison, that you may be tested, and you will have tribulation ten days. Be faithful until death, and I will give you the crown of life …"

H. A. Ironside says the name of this church also has a meaning in Greek.

---

[8] Henrietta C. Mears, *What the Bible Is all About* (Ventura, CA.: Gospel Light Publications, 1966), 651.

Smyrna means "myrrh" [and] myrrh had to
be crushed in order to give out its fragrance.
This sets forth the period when the church was
crushed beneath the iron heel of pagan Rome,[9]
yet it never gave out such sweet fragrance to
God as in those two centuries of almost constant
martyrdom.[10]

Henrietta C. Mears writes, "Smyrna [is] the persecuted
church from Diocletion to Constantine."[11] This means it was
between AD 150 to AD 300. Christianity was very severely
persecuted during that time.

As we will see as we go along, this church gets the best rating
as far as having anything wrong with it, although Philadelphia
isn't altogether that bad.

C. Pergamos

The third church era is Pergamos. It is found in Revelation
2:12–17.

And to the angel of the church in Pergamos
write, "these things says He who has the sharp
two-edged sword; 'I know your works, and

---

[9] Stewart C. Easton, *The Western Heritage: From the Earliest Times to the
Present*, 3rd edition (Austin, TX: Holt, Rinehart, & Winston Inc., 1970), 178

[10] Ironside, op. cit., 40.

[11] Mears, op. cit., 653.

where you dwell, where Satan's throne is, And you hold fast to My name, and did not deny My faith even in the days in which Antipas was My faithful martyr, who was killed among you, where Satan dwells.

"'But I have a few things against you, because you have there those who hold the doctrine of Balaam, who taught Balak to put a stumbling block before the children of Israel, to eat things sacrificed to idols, and to commit sexual immorality.

"'Thus you also have those who hold the doctrine of the Nicolatians, which thing I hate.'"

Ironside says that Pergamos is the church started by Constantine, and this is also reiterated in Easton's history book.[12] Ironside writes, "Pergamos has two meanings. It means 'marriage' and 'elevation.' It speaks of the time when the church was elevated to a place of power and was married to the world. It depicts the time when the church and state were united under Constantine and his successors."[13] I believe this era actually started the Roman Catholic Church.

Mears agrees with Ironside when she says, "Pergamos [was] the church under imperial favor—under Constantine."[14] It is

[12] Easton, op. cit., 161.

[13] Ironside, op. cit., 42.

[14] Mears, op. cit., 653.

true that Constantine thought it was his duty to put the church under the power of the state around AD 312. This ended the persecution that permeated the previous era, but it also converted pagan Rome to Christianity. This church history extends from approximately AD 300 to AD 500.

D. Thyatira

The next church era is Thyatira. It is, in essence, the Roman Catholic Church under leadership of the popes. It came about because the Pergamos church never properly dealt with the doctrine of the Nicolatians, which is the belief of having the leadership of the Church as being supreme.

The Thyatira church is found in Revelation 2:18–29.

> And to the angel of the church in Thyatira write, "These things says the Son of God, who has eyes like a flame of fire, and His feet like fine brass: 'I know your works, love, service, faith, and your patience; and as for your works, the last are more than the first.
>
> Nevertheless I have a few things against you, because you allow that woman Jezebel, who calls herself a prophetess, to teach and seduce My servants to commit sexual immorality and eat things sacrificed to idols.
>
> And I gave her time to repent of her sexual immorality, and she did not repent. Indeed I

will cast her into a sick-bed, and those who commit adultery with her into great tribulation, unless they repent of their deeds ...'"

Ironside says of this church,

> Scholars tell us that it comes from two words, one meaning a sacrifice, or incense offering; the other, that which goes on continually. A suggested interpretation, therefore, is "continual sacrifice" ... or the sacrifice of mass or Eucharist. The Roman Catholic priests declare that, in the mass, they offer a continual sacrifice for the sins of the living and the dead.[15]

Mears agrees, writing, Thyatira is "the Papal church—the Dark Ages."[16]

So this church era is the ancient Roman Catholic Church, which dominated from about AD 500 to AD 1500.

E. Sardis

The next church era is Sardis. It is found in Revelation 3:1–6.

> And to the angel of the church in Sardis write, "These things says He who has the seven Spirits

---

[15] Ironside, op. cit., 49–50.

[16] Mears, op. cit., 654.

of God and the seven stars: 'I know your works, that you have a name that you are alive, but you are dead.

"'Be watchful and strengthen the things which remain, that are ready to die, for I have not found your works perfect before God.

"'Remember how you have received and heard; hold fast and repent. Therefore if you will not watch, I will come upon you as a thief, and you will not know what hour I will come upon you …'"

Ironside says that Sardis means,

> "a remnant," or "those who have escaped" … It brings before us, prophetically, the great state-churches of the reformation, who escaped from Rome … it is plainly to be seen, from the first verse that there is a measure of return to early principles. [17]

And Mears says much the same thing: "the Reformation church—Protestantism, 16th and 17th centuries."[18]

The last one-third of Revelation 3:1 says, "I know your works, that you have a name that you are alive, but you are dead." Does this amply describe our mainline Protestant

---

[17] Ironside, op. cit., 60.

[18] Mears, op. cit., 654.

denominations? Yes, and they escaped from Rome only to fall into the deadness they experience today.

F.   Philadelphia

Because of what was said about the Sardis church, a new church era was necessary, and it is called the Philadelphia church. It is found in Revelation 3:7–13.

> And to the angel of the church in Philadelphia write, "These things says He who is holy, He who is true, 'He who has the key of David, He who opens and no one shuts, and shuts and no one opens': I know your works. See, I have set before you an open door, and no one can shut it; for you have a little strength, have kept My word, and have not denied My name … '"

Ironside says that "this … brings us to what we may call the revival period … In the 18th and 19th centuries, there came over all those lands where the Reformation had gone a great wave of blessing."[19] Mears says it is "the missionary church period ushered in by the Puritan movement."[20]

Ironside and Mears are correct in their assessments about this church era. They are a "wave of blessing" and include all the independent, New Testament churches (independent, that

---

[19]   Ironside, op. cit., p. 66.

[20]   Mears, op. cit., 654.

is, from the mainline Protestant denominations) that reek with love for everyone.[21] These are our late twentieth and early twenty-first century "praise churches." They can be found in any denomination, as well as be independent.

However, cults need not apply. They do more harm than good.

G. Laodicea

Our last church era is Laodicea, which is found in Revelation 3:14–22.

> And to the angel of the church of the Laodiceans write: "These things says the Amen, the Faithful and True Witness, the Beginning of the creation of God: 'I know your works, that you are neither cold or hot. I could wish you were cold or hot.
>
> "'So then, because you are luke-warm, and neither cold nor hot, I will vomit you out of My mouth.
>
> "'Because you say, 'I am rich, have become wealthy, and have need of nothing'—and do not know that you are wretched, miserable, poor, blind, and naked—I counsel you to buy from Me gold refined in the fire, that you may

---

[21] Philadelphia means "brotherly love" in Greek. Strong, op. cit., item 5359.

73

be rich; and white garments, that you may be clothed, that the shame of your nakedness may not be revealed; and anoint your eyes with eye salve, that you may see ...'"

Ironside says, "Laodicea is a compound word and means 'the rights of the people'."[22] In other words, it is when people go their own way and end up in apostasy, This is because they do not have the Spirit of God in their lives, and would rather 'do their own thing' (Jude 19; Isa. 55:8,9; Prov. 12:15; 16:2). Mears agrees, writing, "Laodicea is the rejected church—the church of the final apostasy."[23]

This church goes into the tribulation period and falls under the auspices of the False Prophet after the rapture (Rev. 17:18; 19:20; 13:11–18). It exists parallel with the Philadelphia church for a while, because, it must be remembered, "the mystery of iniquity is already at work" (2 Thess. 2:7a). This being the case, it is already among us, and I believe, it is the ecumenical church.

The apostasy that is associated with this church is brought about by bad doctrines, doctrines that are the result of thinking everything you come up with is the right thing to advocate (Prov. 16:2; 21:2). Three of these doctrines are thinking baptism is the only way to heaven, thinking church membership is the door to heaven, and thinking if our good works outweigh our bad works we will get to heaven.

---

[22] Ironside, op. cit., 68.

[23] Mears, op. cit., 654.

However, we as born-again believers know Jesus Christ is the only way to heaven (Jn. 14:6). He is the door to heaven (Jn. 10:9). There is no way our good works will get us to heaven if Jesus Christ does not live within us (Eph. 2:8, 9; Rom. 3:10-18). This means accepting Jesus Christ into your life—and Him only—constitutes salvation (Jn. 14:6). So we must look for churches with leadership that preaches the Word of God and avoid those that don't (Matt. 16:6; 1 Cor. 5:6; Matt. 13:29–30; 7:15–23).

III. The Significance of the Seven Churches as They Relate to Individual Church Personalities

The seven churches of Revelation, chapters 2 and 3, are also indicative of church personality types that can be seen among the local churches on earth. For example, there have been churches that were once known for being powerhouses at preaching the Word of God, but then they fell into worrying about how they were going to make ends meet. They still preached the Word of God correctly, but it was no longer the first priority in the hearts of church leadership. Financial matters led them to devote much of their time to fund-raising, when a lot of prayer would have done what was necessary. These are Ephesian churches, where they have left their "first love" (Rev. 2:4). The first love of which is 'resting in Jesus' for all your needs (Matt.11:28-30).

Then there are those churches with a pastor who brings a bad doctrine into the pulpit. Since church membership does not know this is the case, the doctrine is adopted as orthodox. This is a Thyatira church situation.

There are also churches that are depending on their laurels. This kind of thing only causes them to grow cold and dead, so these would be Sardis churches.

The reason Sardis churches get so set in their ways is that they get lazy and think that their extreme love for each other and all of humankind will bring everybody 'into the Kingdom'. It is true, loving everybody is a good way to be (1 Jn. 4:7, 11), but we must also preach the word of God fervently (Rom. 10:13, 14).

Some churches backslide to a place of enormous lethargy. These are, in essence, the Loadicean churches. The backsliding includes, for the most part, leaving the doctrine of accepting Jesus Christ as Savior and Lord (Jn. 1:12). So there is no way of finding out about being born again (Jn. 3:7) to enter heaven (Jn. 3:3) in these churches.

On a positive note, we have churches that use all the technological advantages at their disposal to plant seeds of faith in Jesus Christ. These are Pergamos churches, because they marry worldly things to the church.

Then there are persecuted churches, like Smyrna. There have been a few of these lately in America, because the government wanted to examine their tax-exempt status. This generally only brings sympathy for the churches experiencing persecution.

And last, we have Philadelphia churches. Even though the Word of God says they "have a little faith," they are consistently winning people to Jesus Christ. We can rejoice that they are doing this, because this is our calling (Matt. 28:19, 20).

CHAPTER 12

∞

The Individuals,
Establishments, and Events
of the Tribulation Period

The tribulation period which is found from Revelation 6:1 to 18:24, as well as Daniel 11:36–45, consists of individuals, establishments, and events Satan uses to have full control of the earth during this period.

I. The Individuals of the Tribulation Period

A. The Two Beasts

Two individuals are explained in chapter 13 of the book of Revelation and depicted as separate beasts. One is a beast that rises "up out of the sea" (13:1), and the other comes "up out of the earth" (13:11). A significant thing that can be seen when studying the texts pertaining to these two beasts is that the beast coming out of the sea has ten horns, and the beast coming out of the earth has two horns.

1. The Beast That Comes Out of the Sea with Ten Horns

The first beast mentioned in Revelation, chapter 13, comes out of the sea and has ten horns. That this beast comes out of the sea is significant, because it portrays the 'sea of nations.' As John F. Walvoord has written, "The fact that the beast rises out of the sea is taken by many to indicate that he comes from the great mass of humanity, namely the Gentile powers of the world."[24]

Merrill Unger while commenting on Revelation, chapter thirteen, has said about this beast,

> The beast [has a] wicked career, 6–10. He blasphemes God and those who are His, (6). To this end he wars against the saints, (7a) (Dan. 7:21–22; Rev. 11:7, 12). He is permitted unrestrained power over all earth dwellers except over the elect, (8–10) (c.f. Mt. 24:13, 22). He is the antichrist, the man of sin (2 Thess. 2:3–12; 1 Jn. 2:22, 4:3).[25]

As we will see as we go along, the book of Daniel is a parallel book to the book of Revelation. So this beast is also found there in Daniel 11:36-39 where he is militarily inclined among other things.

---

[24] John F. Walvoord, *The Revelation of Jesus Christ (A Commentary by John F. Walvoord)* (Chicago. IL: Moody Press, 1974), 198.

[25] Unger, op. cit., 863.

The horns of this beast are ten "kings" that give their power to the beast (Rev. 17:12). This beast is the Antichrist, who has the whole world in his grip (Rev. 13:3, 4).

2. The Beast That Comes Out of the Earth with Two Horns

The second beast in Revelation, chapter thirteen, has two horns and comes out of the earth. The phrase "from the earth" depicts that false religion, from ancient times to the present, has always "worshipped the creation more than the Creator" (Rom. 1:25), so it is actually the earth that is being worshipped. Hence, this beast comes "up out of the earth."

Walvoord writes,

> The reference to the second beast as coming out of the earth indicates that this character, who is later described as a false prophet (Rev. 19:20), is a creature of earth rather than heaven … He is pictured [here] as having two horns like a lamb and as speaking like a dragon. The description of him as a lamb seems to indicate that he has a religious character, a conclusion supported by his being named a prophet. His speaking as a dragon indicates that he is motivated by the power of Satan who is "the dragon." [26]

---

[26] Walvoord, op. cit., 205.

This second beast also causes the whole earth to worship the first beast by doing miraculous things (Rev. 13:12–15). This being the case, he is the international False Prophet of the end times.

It could also be that the two horns of this beast are the two facets of false religion of the future: Christian and non-Christian. This is how he is able to encompass the whole earth with a false spiritual power. He includes everybody.[27]

B. Two Other Ways of Describing the Two Beasts

In Revelation 17:3, there is a woman called Mystery: Babylon the Great, the Mother of Harlots and of the Abominations of the Earth.[28] She is sitting on "a bright red beast covered with insulting names." [29] The two individuals in this verse will be seen to be as follows.

---

[27] See section II, item G. of chapter 11 (as also section II and item C. of chapter 8) where the ecumenical church of the end times is seen to be prevalent during this time in history. It is commonly thought the False Prophet is the leader of this church after it encompasses all religions of the world (see Rev. 17:15).

[28] This portrayal of this beast is found in The New King James Version of the Bible, (Nashville: Thomas Nelson Publishers, 1992).

[29] The portrayal of this beast is found in God's Word: Today's Bible Translation that Says What It Means (Orange Park, Fla.: God's Word to the Nations Bible Society, 1995).

1. The Bright Red Beast Covered with Insulting Names

Because this beast is constantly blaspheming God, He has named him "Covered with Insulting Names."

Concerning this beast, Daniel 11:36 says, "Then the king shall do according to his own will: he shall exalt and magnify himself above every god, shall speak blasphemies against the God of gods, and shall prosper till the wrath has been accomplished. . ." Since this is the case, the bright red beast is the Antichrist.

2. Mystery Babylon, also Known as a Harlot

While commenting on Revelation 17:1–12, the *Wycliffe Bible Commentary* says Babylon is

> some vast spiritual system that persecutes the saints of God, betraying that to which she was called. She enters into relations with the governments of this earth, and for a while rules them. I think the closest we can come to an identification … is to understand this harlot as symbolic of a vast spiritual power arising at the end of the age which enters into a league with the world and compromises with the worldly forces. Instead of being spiritually true she

is spiritually false, and thus exercises an evil influence in the name of religion.[30]

Again, this is a description of the False Prophet and the worldwide false religion over which he has control. The harlot rules for a while, but as we see in Revelation 17:16–17, she is destroyed by the ten horns. Then the red-colored beast rules alone.

C. Summary

We have seen the beast that comes out of the sea has been named "a bright red beast covered with insulting names" and is the Antichrist. And we have seen the beast that comes from the earth has been named a "harlot" and is the False Prophet. In this section we see the Antichrist as a person who totally hates God and has the whole world under his control (Rev. 13:3). We also see the False Prophet as having control of the one-world religious system during the tribulation period.

II. The Establishments of the Tribulation Period

Both the Antichrist and the False Prophet have establishments that help them gain full control of the world population. To understand how they received these establishments, we must examine two dreams in the book of Daniel.

---

[30] *The Wycliffe Bible Commentary,* edited by Charles F. Pfeiffer, Old Testament; and Everett F. Harrison, New Testament (Nashville, TN: The Southwestern Company, 1962), 1,517.

A. The Dreams of Nebuchadnezzar and Daniel

Both Nebuchadnezzar and Daniel have dreams described in the book of Daniel. Nebuchadnezzar dreamed the first one, found in Daniel 2:31–35, and Daniel's dream is told in Daniel 7:2–14.

1. Nebuchadnezzar's Dream

Daniel 2: 31–35 tells of Nebuchadnezzar's dream, as does verses 37-45 tell of the interpretation of the dream. It is about a statue with a head of gold, chest and arms of silver, stomach and thighs of bronze, legs of iron, and feet partly of iron and partly of clay. He also dreamed that "the God of heaven will set up a kingdom which shall never be destroyed" in verses 44 and 45. This latter is the millennial kingdom of Jesus Christ (Zech. 2:8-10; Rev. 20:2-5).

Daniel 2:38 says the head of gold is Nebuchadnezzar. So this part of the statue refers to ancient Babylon, of which Nebuchadnezzar was king. Verse 39 speaks of "another kingdom," arising after Nebuchadnezzar. This would be the silver part of the statue which is Media-Persia according to Daniel 8:20. Daniel 2:39 also speaks of a "third Kingdom of bronze," and according to Daniel 8:21 is ancient Greece. And verse 40 describes the fourth kingdom as being "strong as iron," and is the ancient Roman Empire.

But in Daniel 2:34, 35, as well as in 2:44, 45, the stone "cut out without hands, which struck the image on its feet of iron and clay, and broke them in pieces" is speaking of Jesus Christ.

And as we will see, it is also He who destroys the fourth beast of Daniel's dream in the future.

2. Daniel's Dream

Daniel's dream, told in Daniel 7:2–14, had four beasts in it. Daniel 7:3 says, "And four great beasts came up from the sea, each different from the other."

The first beast is found in Daniel 7:4: "The first was like a lion and had eagle's wings. I watched till its wings were plucked off; and it was lifted up from the earth, and made to stand on two feet as a man, and a man's heart was given to it."

Stewart C. Easton, in his book *The Western Heritage: From the Earliest Times to the Present,* says that Babylon was like a lion in its dealings with Israel and the takeover of the world, [31] so this beast is ancient Babylon.

Henrietta C. Mears, in her book *What the Bible Is All About,* writes, "The first, or Babylon, was like a lion with eagle's wings, [and this speaks of its swiftness in battle (see Jeremiah 49:22)]"[32]

The second beast is found in Daniel 7:5: "And suddenly another beast, a second, like a bear. It was raised up on one side, and had three ribs in its mouth between its teeth. And they said thus unto it: 'arise, devour much flesh!'" That this beast is ancient Media–Persia is exemplified by the fact that the

---

[31] Easton, op. cit., 37–44.

[32] Mears, op. cit., 267.

three ribs are Media, Babylon[33], and Persia, which was formed about this time by Cyrus, the Median king, after he conquered the other two.[34] Mears says that "Persia was the bear, the cruel animal who delights to kill for the sake of killing." [35] Easton says the Media-Persians were gruesome fighters always ready to go to war with their neighbors.[36]

The third beast is described in Daniel 7:6: "After this I looked, and there was another, like a leopard, which had on its back four wings of a bird. The beast also had four heads, and dominion was given to it." This beast is ancient Greece under the leadership of Alexander the Great, because it was given dominion over the whole known world at that time by his efforts.[37] Again I quote from Mears: "The third [beast] was a leopard or panther, a beast of prey. His four wings portray swiftness. Here we see the rapid marches of Alexander's army and his insatiable love of conquest."[38]

Also, the number four is mentioned twice in the biblical text, which denotes the division of ancient Greece into four parts.[39] (We find this also in Daniel 11:4). These four sections

---

[33] Babylon was in co-rulership with Media at this time in history (see Easton, op. cit., 44, 53).

[34] Ibid., 44, 53.

[35] Mears, op. cit., 267.

[36] Easton, op. cit., 45.

[37] Ibid., 101–104.

[38] Mears, op. cit., 267, 268.

[39] Easton, op. cit., 101–104.

each had a governor, which corresponds to the four heads in our text.

The fourth, and last, beast is described in Daniel 7:7. It reads, "After this I saw in the night visions, and behold, a fourth beast, dreadful and terrible, exceedingly strong. It had huge iron teeth; it was devouring, braking in pieces, and trampling the residue with its feet. It was different from all the beasts that were before it, and it had ten horns."

This beast is certainly a terrible beast, because the text indicates it devoured and conquered everything in the world, and everything felt its iron rule. [40] Because of these things, this last beast is thought to be ancient Rome.

Mears only says that "The fourth beast was different from all the rest." [41] One of the reasons this beast is so different is that it has toes of mixed iron and clay. This is portrayed in Daniel 2:40–43.

> And the fourth kingdom shall be strong as iron, inasmuch as iron breaks in pieces, and shatters everything; and like iron that crushes, that kingdom, will break in pieces and crush all the others. Whereas you saw the feet and toes, partly of potter's clay and partly of iron, the kingdom shall be divided; yet the strength of the iron shall be in it, just as you saw the iron mixed with ceramic clay. And as the toes of the

---

[40] Easton, op. cit., 118-162.

[41] Mears, op. cit., 268.

feet were partly of iron and partly of clay, so the kingdom shall be partly strong, and partly fragile. As you saw iron mixed with ceramic clay, they will mingle with the seed of men; but they will not adhere one to another, just as iron does not mix with clay.

The significance of this mixture of iron and clay that doesn't adhere to each other pictures how things have been since the time of the ancient Roman Empire. Many countries now make up the territory that once occupied that area, and they really don't like to cooperate together.

3.   What Is Learned from These Two Dreams

As can be seen, the two dreams parallel each other. They both have four earthly kingdoms: Babylon, Media-Persia, Ancient Greece, and the Roman Empire. Both tell the story in which the last one is destroyed by Jesus Christ.

However, it is commonly thought the fourth beast turns into the revived Roman Empire (i.e. "deadly wound is healed" in Revelation 13:3). It also turns into a one-world government, because it is an all-encompassing world-wide power. This is found in Revelation 17:9–11.

Here is the mind which has wisdom: The seven heads are seven mountains on which the woman sits. There are also seven kings. Five have fallen, one is, and the other has not yet come. And when he comes, he must continue a short time. The beast that was, and is not, is himself also the eighth, and is of the seven, and is going to perdition.

But these mountains are not speaking of the city of Rome, or even Jerusalem. Instead, they refer to seven imperialist world governments. Of this, John F. Walvoord writes,

> The seven heads of the beast ... are said to be symbolic of seven kings described in verse 10. Five of these are said to have fallen, one is in contemporary existence, that is, in John's lifetime, the seventh is yet to come and will be followed by another described as the eighth, which is the beast itself. In the Greek there is no word for "there," thus translated literally, the phrase is "and are seven kings." The seven heads are best explained as referring to seven kings who represent seven successive forms of the kingdom ... [Scripture] does not say, "the seven heads are seven mountains, where the woman sits upon them" and there leave off; but [it] adds immediately, "and they are seven kings," or personified kingdoms. The mountains, then,

are not piles of material rocks and earth at all, but royal or imperial powers.[42]

Revelation 17:10 speaks of the ancient Roman Empire as the sixth of all these encompassing world powers (i.e., "one is"). But the dreams only speak of four of them. The answer to this is that there were two world powers before Babylon. They are: the Egyptian Empire and the Assyrian Empire.

In his book *Unleashing the Beast* Perry Stone writes,

> Both past and future biblical prophecy is always linked to Israel and the Jewish people. Of the seven prophetic kings, John, when writing the book of Revelation, indicated that five had already fallen and no longer existed in John's time. These kingdoms began with the Egyptian Empire, which was the first major empire in the Bible to impact the Hebrew people for more than four hundred years (Gen. 15:13). These five kingdoms included: [the Egyptian Empire, the Assyrian Empire, the Babylonian Empire, the Medo-Persian Empire, and the Greek Empire.][43]

However, our text in Revelation 17:9-11 speaks of not only the Roman Empire as the one that was in existence in John's

---

[42] Walvoord, op. cit., 251–254.

[43] Perry Stone, *Unleashing the Beast* (Lake Mary, FL: Front Line Charisma Media/Charisma House, 2009–2011), 21, 22.

day, but of another one that has "not yet come" as the seventh beast. This is speaking of the revival of the Roman Empire.

Leon Wood is another theologian who believes from the evidence presented in the book of Daniel that there will be a revival of the Roman Empire. While commenting on the fourth beast of Daniel 7:8, he writes,

> The correct view [of this] can only be that there will be a time still future when the Roman empire will be restored ... a time when ten contemporary kings will rule, among whom another will arise, uprooting three in the process, and then move on to become the head of all ... the new horn must symbolize another king, like the others, only emerging later, though while they still rule. Because the description of this ruler, given in this verse and later in verses twenty-four to twenty-six, corresponds to descriptions of the "beast" of Revelation 13:5–8 and 17:11–14, the two are correctly identified. The one so described is commonly and properly called the Antichrist, who will be Satan's counterfeit world ruler, trying to preempt the place of God's true world ruler, Jesus Christ, who will later establish His reign during the millennium.[44]

---

[44] Leon Wood, *A Commentary on Daniel* (Grand Rapids, MI: Zondervan, 1973), 187–188.

Not only is the Roman Empire revived, but a strong leader emerges from it to become the ruler of the one-world government (Rev. 13:4, 8; 17:12; Dan. 7:24). And, as Revelation 17:11 says, this strong leader is the Antichrist (i.e. "the beast that was, and is not" referring to when he tried to set up his kingdom through Nimrod in Genesis, Chapter 11, as well as other despots such as Nebuchadnezzar). It is he who sets up his own evil empire. Who this is has not yet been revealed, and it won't be until after the rapture of the church (2 Thess. 2:8).

B. Other Entities in the Tribulation Period

1. Magog

There is a strong nation called Magog mentioned in chapters 38 and 39 of the book of Ezekiel. It is from "the uttermost northern parts" of the world (Ezek. 39:2), and it is believed to be modern-day Russia. How do we know that "Gog, of the land of Magog, the prince of Rosh, Meshech, and Tubal" (Ezek. 38:2) is speaking of a leader of Russia? There are several ways of knowing. One would be to trace Noahic ancestry in Genesis 10:2–5 to those who settled in the northern parts of the world. For example, Noahic genealogists generally agree that Tubal is the same as the region of Tubalsk, and Mesheck is the same as Moscow.

But another reason Magog is thought to be Russia is that many biblical scholars feel this way. The *Wycliffe Bible Commentary* says, "These chapters describe in apocalyptic manner God's deliverance of His people from an unparalleled invasion by a dreadful foe … an invasion previously predicted ([Ezek.] 38:17; 39:8) … made by nations dwelling in the outskirts of the world."[45]

Unger writes, "The Great Last-Day Northern Confederacy, [Ezek.] 38:1–6, Gog is the leader of the coalition … Magog [is] his land. . . [This is in] the general area [that is] now occupied by Russia ('the uttermost parts of the north')."[46] It also fits contemporary thought that a bear comes out of the north and attacks Israel, and I feel this happens in Daniel 11:22, 30.[47]

Magog also has a few allies. As found in Ezekiel 38:5, 6, they are Persia, or Iran; Ethiopia; Libya; Gomer, or Turkey; and Togarmah, or Georgia and Armenia.

I believe this conglomeration of Russia and its allies will be defeated "on the mountains of Israel" (Ezek. 39:1–6) and that it takes place near the beginning of the great tribulation. This is why the Antichrist is able to make a covenant with Israel (Dan. 9:27).

2. Edom (or, Mt. Seir):

According to Ezekiel, chapter 35 (and Psalm 137:7, as well as Jeremiah 49:7-11) there is the presence of a strong nation southeast of Israel. It is called Mt. Seir, or Edom, and would be the "king of the south" of Daniel, chapter eleven.

---

[45] Wycliffe, op. cit.,755.

[46] Unger, op. cit., 378.

[47] It is still the king of the North that is prevalent here until verse 29. It then changes to the Antichrist. (It is true this is speaking of Antiochus Epiphanes but history repeats itself. It is also why so much time is given to the episode here in Daniel 11.)

Of this Unger says, "Mt. Seir is the plateau east of Arabah in which Sela (Petra), the Edomite capital, was located."[48] It is also where Saudi Arabia is located.

In Daniel 11:5-35 two kings are constantly warring against each other. Most commentaries agree that these are the Ptolemies and the Seleucids. Wood says while commenting on Daniel 11:5-20,

> Having predicted that there would be four divisions to Alexander's empire, the angel continued to speak of only two: the Syrian division, lying just north of Palestine, over which the Seleucid line of kings would rule; and the Egyptian division, lying just south, over which the Ptolemaic line would be supreme.[49]

As also the *Wycliffe Bible Commentary* says, "[the] Prophecy of Syria and Egypt in Conflict with One Another . . ."[50]

But why give so much attention to this in Scripture? It is because this is a picture of things to come. It is when Syria and its allies, or "the king of the north" and also a strong southern nation (southern in that it is south of Israel) and its allies are in conflict with each other.

---

[48] Unger, op. cit., 377.

[49] Wood, op. cit., 283.

[50] Wycliffe, op. cit., 797.

Could it be that this is the beginning of the 'Magog' ordeal? Daniel, chapter 11 has "the king of the north" as a very strong personage. I think he then, along with his allies, joins the leader of Russia to invade Israel.

3. Rumors About Magog and the Kings of the East

In Daniel 11:44, the Antichrist hears rumors from the east and the north.

However, the "north" in Daniel 11:44 is not the same person as" the king of the north" we mentioned in the previous section. Here in Daniel 11:44, it is "tidings" or a pieces of information that disturbs the Antichrist. So it is at this time that the planning for the invasion of Israel by Magog takes place, and soon the "bear" coming out from the north will attack Israel. The Antichrist hears about this planning that is being done, and it does not make him happy.

4. Kings of the East

In Revelation 16:12, the way is made for "kings of the east" to come across the Euphrates River, and I feel it is they who are being mentioned in Daniel 11:44 as the "east." China, Japan, and South Korea, as well as India could sometime in the future conglomerate together to become one of the ten kings of Revelation 17:12, so they could come to Armageddon as one unit (Rev. 16:14b).

I don't know why they disturb the Antichrist in Daniel 11:44. It could be just the fact that they have strong economies that can support large armies.

5. The United States

In Daniel 11:30, the "ships of Chittim" come against the Antichrist. "Ships of Chittim" usually refers to what is now the island of Cyprus. But Cyprus is not a world-class contender for hindering an evil empire bent on taking over the world. It is, instead, generally thought it is the United States being spoken of here, because we are included as "those who are living carelessly in the isles" (Ezek. 39:6 in KJV). It must be remembered that we are also known as "a young lion" of England in Ezekiel 38:13, and England is one of those "isles" whose inhabitants are living carelessly.

6. The Ten-Member Conglomeration

Whenever the number ten is mentioned in the book of Daniel or the book of Revelation, it seems to refer to the ten-member confederation of the last days (Dan. 7:7, 24; Rev. 17:12). This ten-member confederation is said to be a revived Roman-like empire. It is also the seventh world empire (Rev. 17:10–11).

I believe this ten-member conglomeration is more than just a united Europe; it is worldwide in scope. However, a united Europe could be the one who spawns, assembles, and promotes this seventh world power. This is because, it is generally agreed, the "deadly wound" healed in Revelation 13:3 refers to the healing and revival of the Roman Empire, which will have its headquarters somewhere in Europe.

Europe will work more in concert with the United Nations in the future, with the United Nations becoming stronger every day as the world's police force. Many people think this should be the case, rather than the United States serving that purpose.

7. The Three Superpowers

Three superpowers must be conquered by the Antichrist before he takes over the ten-member conglomeration (Dan. 7:8, 24). But I think he does this by humbling them financially and taking over their economies.

The three economic superpowers in the world right now are: the United States, China and Japan. But who they will be in the future remains to be seen.

III. The Events of the Tribulation Period

There are many events that take place during the tribulation period some of which we will examine at this time.

A. Antichrist Revealed

The first thing that happens is the rapture, and then the great tribulation starts (2 Thess. 2:7). It is after this that the Antichrist is revealed, as it says in 2 Thessalonians 2:8.

B. A United World Comes into Being

As was mentioned earlier, a ten-member conglomeration of nations (Rev. 17: 3, 12; 13:1; Dan. 7:7) comes on the scene that ultimately gives its power to the Anti-Christ (Rev. 17:13). We have seen that this will be the seventh world power in history (Rev. 17:9-11). And we also saw that it is the world uniting under the leadership of Europe who lets the Antichrist take over. He then establishes a totalitarian regime such as never been seen since the establishment of the world (Dan. 7:19-21; 12:1; Matt. 24:9-29)[51] as the eighth world-wide regime.

Right now globalization is in the forefront, so the stage is being set up for this.

C. The Covenant Made with Israel

Daniel 9:27 tells of a covenant made between Israel and the Antichrist, with the leader of Israel being called "the prince of the covenant" in Daniel 11:22. This leader of Israel is a renegade Caananite (Gen. 9:25-27) posing as a Jew, which is how he hoodwinks Israel into signing a peace pact with the Antichrist.

This takes place directly after the Magog war near the beginning of the tribulation period. Settling this conflict is

---

[51] Nazi Germany was about as terrible as anything the modern world has ever seen, however, you can't imagine how terrible this eighth regime will be under the Antichrist (Jer. 30:5-7; Amos 5:16-20). It will be much worse, because the Antichrist is not demon possessed, he is Satan possessed (Rev. 13:2).

why the Antichrist is able to make the pact with Israel after he defeats the Arab–Magog union.

D. Magog and Arab Nations Attack the Antichrist

Sometime after the great tribulation begins, Magog and the king of the North and the King of the South, in concert with a host of Arab nations, attack the Antichrist (Dan. 11:40a,b). This also makes him very angry (Dan. 11:40c).

E. The United States Asks a Question

We have seen the United States is being spoken of as "a young lion" of "those who are living carelessly in the isles" in Ezekiel 39:6. Also they are seen as "the ships of Chittim" in Daniel 11:30.

However, all we are able to do when Russia and her allies attack Israel near the beginning of the tribulation is to ask them, "Are you invading Israel to plunder it (Ezek. 38:13)?" But it is good to know we at least still have enough resolve to want to know what Russia is doing to Israel.

Israel has enough resolve to fight back against the Magog invasion. This is found in Psalm 83 and Ezekiel 39:4,5.

F. The Antichrist, and the False Prophet, Have Full Support of the Inhabitants of the World

The Antichrist and the False Prophet have the full support of the inhabitants of the world (Rev. 13:3c) after the Antichrist takes over as the eighth world power. One of the ways he does this is to establish a one-world economic system found in Revelation 13:16–18. It is the False Prophet who is in charge of this worldwide economic system (Rev. 13:12, 16, 17), because he is able to convince as many as possible "to receive a mark on their right hand or on their foreheads" (Rev. 13:16). He is able to do this because he uses his power as a bully pulpit.

G. The Covenant Desecrated by the Abomination of Desolation

The covenant that has been made between Israel and the Antichrist near the beginning of the tribulation is broken in the middle of the tribulation (Dan. 9:27; 8:11; 12:11).[52] The Antichrist is very angry because of the war he had to engage in with the United States in Daniel 11:30. So in verse 31, he desecrates and nullifies the covenant to appease his bruised ego. This event is called the "abomination of desolation" (Dan. 12:11; Matt. 24:15; Mk. 13:14).

H. The Occupation of Israel

The occupation of Israel is seen in Daniel 11:30–32, as well as in Daniel 11:41 and 45. This happens near the beginning of the tribulation period (Dan. 12:11; Rev. 12:6) after the Magog war. It is also after the covenant is made with the Antichrist.

---

[52] Weeks in eschatology are actually years.

But those Israelites who find God's favor will be hidden "in the wilderness" (Dan 12:1c, d; Rev. 12:6, 14).

I. The Four Horsemen of Revelation Come on the scene

The four horsemen mentioned in Revelation 6:2–8 allegorically represent events that happen at the beginning of the tribulation period. For example, the white horseman represents the Antichrist, because even though he looks like a savior of humankind, he is in actuality a deceiver. Although he appears to be for peace (Dan. 11:21, 24, 27, 28), he is actually for war. Likewise, the red horse represents the wars the Antichrist brings with him (Dan. 11:28-31). The black horse is the famine that war always brings with it. And the pale horse is widespread pestilence, as well as death.

So as it can be seen from these representative figures, the tribulation period is not a good time for humanity or beasts.

J. The Two Halves of the Tribulation

The Great Tribulation has two halves, each approximately three and a half years in length (Dan. 7:25; 12:11).

Revelation 6:1-11 and Daniel 7:25 speak of things the Antichrist does in the first half of the tribulation period. Daniel 9:27 c,d, along with Revelation 6:12-17 and, chapters 8, 9, and 16, speak of things that happen in the second half of the tribulation.

That the second half of the tribulation is a horrible time for humankind is confirmed in Daniel 12:1, where it says, "and there shall be a time of trouble, such as never was since there was a nation." Needless to say, things really get tough for humankind during this time in history. In fact, it can really be said this is the judgment of the gentiles.[53]

K. The Trumpet and Bowl Judgments

In the second half of the tribulation humankind must endure the sixth seal (Rev. 6:12-17), the trumpets (Rev. 8:6–9:21; 11:15-19) and the bowl (Rev. 15:1–16:21) judgments.

The seals, trumpets and bowl judgments are like fireworks, in that the next one comes out of the seventh. In other words, they come out of the former in the form of explosions, so that the seventh seal (Rev. 8:1) is actually the trumpet judgments, and the seventh trumpet (Rev. 11:15–19) is actually the bowl judgments. So they intensify and are a lot like the plagues of Exodus 7:17–12:33.

L. The Euphrates River Dries Up

Revelation 16:12 tells of the drying up of the Euphrates river. About this, Walvoord writes, "The purpose of the drying up of the Euphrates is indicated as a preparation for 'the way of the kings of the east' … The passage is best understood as referring

---

[53] It is judgment for the gentiles, because a remnant of Israel is hidden away from all this (Rev. 12:6, 14; Dan.12:12).

to ... Oriental rulers who will descend upon the Middle East in connection with the final world conflict described a few verses later."[54]

This drying up of the Euphrates is also referred to in Isaiah 11:15, 16 and Zechariah 10:11. But why dry up the Euphrates River? Scripture says it is to help "gather" the world to Armageddon (Rev. 16:13-16; 19:19).

M. Armageddon

The battle of Armageddon is found in Daniel 11:45b, Zechariah 12:2,3; 14:2–4, and Revelation 16:13-16; 19:19.

While commenting on Revelation 16:16, Walvoord writes,

> . . . it reflects a conflict among the nations themselves in the latter portion of the great tribulation as the world empire so hastily put together begins to disintegrate. The armies of the world contending for honors on the battlefield at the very time of the second coming of Christ do all turn, however, and combine their efforts against Christ and His army from heaven when the glory of the second coming appears in the heavens. [55]

N. The Glorious Second Coming of Jesus Christ

---

[54] Walvoord, op. cit., 236.

[55] Ibid., 237

When Jesus Christ returns (Rev. 19:11–15a), all He has to do is start speaking, and that great war called Armageddon crumbles. (Actually, it never really happens, because all that is ever said is everybody is "gathered around Jerusalem," and Jesus puts a stop to it.)

It is at this time the Antichrist and the False Prophet are captured and put into the lake of fire. Everybody else is killed by the words Jesus says (Rev. 19:20, 21).

Part 3

∞

About Those Spiritual Gifts

CHAPTER 13

※

Introduction

When I wrote chapter 5, it became so large I had to take a big portion of it and make it into another section. It is now this section, Part 3. It is very evident the Lord had much to teach me, and I have thoroughly enjoyed it. I pray that you will, too!

At this time there will be a thorough listing of the gifts of the Holy Spirit, so that there will be no confusion as to how to manifest them. I also give a few warnings against manifesting spiritual gifts in the wrong way. It is important for gifts to be manifested correctly, because many people do not appreciate the wrong manifestation of them (1 Cor. 14:11, 23). This is because it goes against graceful behavior to do so (1 Cor. 14:33; 13:1-3).

I have also included a chapter about whether any of the spiritual gifts have ceased. There are many aspects to this, because there are partial cessationists, total cessationists, and those who do not feel anything has ceased. Early in my born-again life, I wondered who was right. So I embarked on a thorough study of the spiritual gifts to find out which ones were still in effect.

I also worked on the premise that even though there was the false, there had to be the real thing for there to be the false. A member of the ape family can mimic a human being, but just because he mimics the human doesn't mean the human doesn't exist. There are those who would say that "well, the spiritual gifts are all being manifested falsely, so spiritual gifts don't exist anymore." This is not true, as we will see in chapter 15.

CHAPTER 14

❧

Three Erroneous Things
Associated with Spiritual Gifts

People do three erroneous things when they try to manifest spiritual gifts.

I.   Calling Attention to the Holy Spirit Himself

When the Holy Spirit is manifested as a spiritual gift, He most of the time does not call attention to Himself (Jn. 16:13,14). Instead, He calls attention to Jesus Christ. Spiritual gifts are not intended to be something by which people glorify themselves (1 Cor. 12:7; 13:1-7). Instead, spiritual gifts are intended to be something that would encourage the speaking to and the serving of one another (1 Pet. 4:10; 1 Cor. 12:18–26; Eph. 4:16).

So spiritual gifts are not for the purpose of seeking selfish motives. In this way, they will not degenerate into excessive emotional displays, incantatory swooning, or unauthorized metaphysical phenomena (1 Cor. 14:32,33; 2 Thess. 2:9,10).

II. Manifesting Spiritual Gifts in the Same Way the False
    Prophet Will Manifest Them during the Tribulation Period

If you try to manifest spiritual gifts in the same way apostolic
signs, wonders, and miracles were manifested, you might end
up with the same thing the False Prophet will manifest during
the tribulation period. This is because the Greek words for
"signs," "wonders," and "miracles" are the same in Hebrews
2:4 as they are in 2 Thessalonians 2:9. The only difference is
that in Hebrews 2:4, they are done "according to [God's] own
will," whereas in 2 Thessalonians 2:9, they are "according to
the working of Satan."

So it is possible to manifest spiritual gifts in the wrong way
(1 Cor. 14:23, 32, 40; 2 Cor. 11:14, 15), which is why limitations
are put on them. In other words, they should be done as chapter
14 of 1 Corinthians indicates, so that unbelievers will not be
turned off by them (see 14:23).

III. Constantly Seeking of the Baptism of the Holy Spirit and
     Gifts of the Holy Spirit

Many people seek the baptism of the Holy Spirit and the gifts
of the Holy Spirit after they are saved. According to the Bible,
this should not be done. In other words, a person shouldn't seek
what has been amply supplied at salvation (Rom. 12:3; Eph.
4:7; 1 Pet. 4:10; Rom. 8:9c).

It is true that 1 Corinthians 12:31 says we should "covet
earnestly" the best gifts. (In the New King James it is "earnestly

desire".) However, the Greek word for "covet" here is *zeloo* [1] which means "to be zealous" and says we should be zealous in using our gifts. *Zeloo* is a derivative of the Greek words *zelos* and *zeo*,[2] which mean "zeal" or "to be fervent." It does not mean to want more.

The Greek term for wanting more is *epithumeo,* which is also used for the phrase "to covet" in other places in the Bible. Its definition is "to lust after"[3] and is not what is meant in 1 Corinthians 12:31. It is found in passages such as Romans 7:7 and Acts 20:33, and when it becomes a noun, it means "a craver."[4]

So we should not crave more gifts after we are saved. There could be times in a person's life when it seems as if he or she is getting more gifts, but in actuality, he or she is merely getting rid of the "self-life" so that God's gifts can shine forth. (This concept is found in Colossians 3:9,10 as well as Romans 8:11,12 and 1 Cor. 5:5.)

When we seek the baptism of the Holy Spirit along with the gifts of the Holy Spirit after we are saved, we are not acting according to Scripture (Rom. 8:9). We should instead realize we were given sufficient gifts at the baptism in the Holy Spirit (1 Cor. 12:7,11-13; Eph. 4:7,8). We should also fervently develop the gifts that were given to us and put them to use.

---

[1] James Strong, *The Exhaustive Concordance of the Bible* (New York and Nashville: Abingdon Press), item 2206 in the Greek dictionary.

[2] Ibid., items 2205 and 2204 respectively.

[3] Ibid., item 1937.

[4] Ibid., item 1938.

CHAPTER 15

◈

The Cessation Found in
1 Corinthians 13:8–12

Does 1 Corinthians 13:8–12 advocate the cessation of spiritual gifts? There are people who believe it does and that some or all spiritual gifts have ceased. But after an in-depth study of this passage, we will see nothing has ceased as far as spiritual gifts are concerned.

The interpretation of this passage hinges on the meaning of two words in 1 Corinthians 13:8-12. They are the word "part" in verses 9, 10, and 12; and the word "perfect" in verse 10. So we shall take an in-depth look at what they mean.

In Greek the word "part" is *meros,* meaning "a division, or share." [5] It is a noun. As also in Hebrews 2:4, the word "gifts" is *merismos* in Greek and means "a distribution." [6] It would be the predicate objective form of meros, and as the three verses prior to Hebrews 2:4 say, it refers to everything that was given in the apostolic period.

In Romans 12:3, God "dealt" to each person a gift. It is *merizo*[7] in Greek and would be the verb form of the other two. This is another example of the word "part" being used to refer

---

[5]   Strong, op. cit., #3313.

[6]   Ibid., item 3311.

[7]   Ibid., item 3307.

to what was given on the day of Pentecost. So the word "part" refers to the apostolic period and the gifts given on Pentecost.

Now to the word "perfect." In verse 10, the word "perfect" is *teleios* in Greek and means "completeness,"[8] or maturity. And it is the desire of God that everyone become mature (Matt. 5:48; 2 Cor. 13:11; Col. 1:28; 4:12), preferably before we die.

But the maturity happening in these verses refers to an event in history, the maturity the Lord brought about near the beginning of the church dispensation. So it refers to the completion of the Bible as we know it, based on the original Greek texts.[9] This being the case, it is not speaking of the end of the church dispensation when Jesus Christ comes back, but the maturity that the Bible brought, because it had everything it needed for doing God's work.

But why does 1 Corinthians 13:8 say that prophecy, tongues, and knowledge has ceased? We know that in Revelation 22:18 if Scripture is added to, error will be in evidence. I have run across people who believe that their preaching and their writings that they do, supposedly by manifesting a spiritual gift, are divinely inspired and therefore are the word of God. But this does not line up with Revelation 22:18. So if the gifts of prophecy, knowledge or tongues are said to add something to the Word of God, the gifts are not being used properly. This means the so called inspired additions are not valid.

---

8 Strong, op. cit., item 5046.

9 The word *teleios* is gender-neutral, so it refers to the Bible, not to Jesus Christ. If it were masculine, it would refer to our Lord.

So it is that aspect that would bring about new revelation that has ceased. [10] And it was the existence of a Divine, inspired, canon of Scripture that brought about the cessation of prophecy and knowledge as meros gifts. This means they now illuminate Scripture instead of write it.

The gift of tongues is also mentioned in verse 8. However, according to the Greek construction, it is a little different. It says they come to cessation by their own accord.[11] But they have not ceased yet. They have only been changed from meros gifts to charisma gifts.

These three gifts have changed their function from revelation giving to the interpretation of the Bible. This is so the gospel will be presented in the proper way

---

[10] In the apostolic period, meros was for the giving of revelation.

[11] In 1 Corinthians 13:8, tongues is in a middle, indicative voice, meaning they come to cessation of their own accord. Knowledge and prophecy are in a passive, indicative voice, meaning that something must bring them to cessation.

It is, therefore, the fact that tongues gradually cease when they are no longer needed—due to the fact that learning foreign languages is getting easier all the time—that brings them to cessation of their own accord. But it is the rapture that finally brings knowledge and prophecy to cessation in the charisma form.

CHAPTER 16

∞

The Spiritual Gifts Listed
and Defined with Their
Greek Definitions

Scripture says that we should not "be ignorant" (1 Cor. 12:1) of spiritual gifts. So we will list them and give Greek definitions for them, along with the English.

In this study, we look at five lists of spiritual gifts found in the New Testament. The three main lists are found in 1 Corinthians 12:8–10, Romans 12:6–8, and Ephesians 4:11. There are also two minor lists found in 1 Corinthians 12:28, as well as 1 Corinthians 14:26.

In addition to this, there are three places that give supportive information for the other five lists. They are 1 Peter 4:11, 2 Corinthians 8:7, and 1 Corinthians 12:4–6.

I.   The Three Main Lists of Spiritual Gifts in the New Testament

The context surrounding each of these lists of spiritual gifts speaks of the "Body of Christ," so those who have these gifts are members of that body (Rom. 12:4, 5; 1 Cor. 12:4–7, 12; Eph. 4:4–7). Therefore, all the gifts listed here can be manifested by

115

the Universal Church anywhere within society. They would not need to wait to be manifested only in the local church.

A. Gifts Found in 1 Corinthians 12:8–10

1. Word of Wisdom.

"Word" is *logos* in Greek and has "communication" as one of its definitions.[12] "Wisdom" is *sophia* in Greek and means as our text says: "wisdom."[13] This being the case, the gift of word of wisdom is the special ability to say wise things while speaking for the Lord.

2. Word of Knowledge.

As before, "word" is *logos* in Greek. "Knowledge" is *gnosis* in Greek and means the same as our text says: "knowledge."[14] Another definition for knowledge is "that which is known."[15] Since the gift of knowledge includes communication—including preaching—it is the special ability to say knowledgeable things while speaking for the Lord.[16]

---

[12] Strong, op. cit., item 3056.

[13] Ibid., item 4678.

[14] Ibid., item 1108.

[15] *The American Heritage Dictionary of the English Language,* op. cit.

[16] Some people say this gift is a means of knowing something about someone in order to minister to them effectively. However, as we will see, that is what ministers do and is the revelation as found in 1 Corinthians 14:26.

3.   Faith.

Faith can have five meanings in English as well as in Greek. They are: the faith found in Hebrews 11:1, which everyone who is born again should have; the whole of Christian character; a pledge or a promise given; reliance on something or someone you believe in; and the whole system of Christian truth.

The Greek word for the gift of faith is *pistis*[17], and is, "the system of religious [or Gospel] truth itself." So, in actuality, it is the fifth definition. This means it is "the special ability to work with everything that pertains to Christian doctrine."[18]

The people who have this gift also have the special ability to go to the Greek for a correct interpretation of what the Bible says. In fact, these people love doing that, while the majority of Christians don't. Another thing these people are sometimes able to do is write systematic theology books.

4.   Gifts of Healing.

The Greek word for healing is *iama* and means "a cure."[19] But it does not necessarily apply only to the healing of the body. As you will notice, the word 'gifts' is plural, so it is also the special ability to work with a person to heal him or her spiritually and emotionally, as well as the healing of the body.

---

[17] Strong, op. cit., item 4102.

[18] The gift of faith is usually said to be the gift of doing mighty work for the Lord. However, as we shall see, that is the gift of working of miracles.

[19] Strong, op. cit., item 2386.

5. Working of Miracles.

The word "working" is *energema*[20] in Greek, the same as the "operations" of 1 Corinthians 12:4. It means being able to do things in God's power. Also, "miracles" is *dunamis* in Greek and means "mighty wonderful work."[21] So the gift of working of miracles is the special ability to do mighty work for the Lord that wouldn't otherwise be done.

6. Prophecy.

The word for prophecy in Greek is *propheteia* and means "a prediction."[22] Closely related to this is *prophetes*,[23] or a prophet. It has two meanings. They are "having insight into divine things and speaking them forth to others," and "to predict." So prophecy has two aspects to it: (1) it is when a person is gifted at speaking, and (2) a kind of a predictive thing that helps us in life.

However, now that revelation through the inspiration of God (2 Tim. 3:16a) has ceased (Rev. 22:18) for our day and age (in other words, for the church dispensation), the gift of prophecy has changed primarily from predictions to speaking forth of the things of God. In the Old Testament there was an element of speaking forth to the gift of prophecy, but it was always in

---

[20] Strong, op. cit., item 1755.

[21] Ibid., item 1411.

[22] Ibid., item 4394. The apostle Paul was given a prophecy not to go to Jerusalem in Acts 21:4. He went anyway and experienced trouble. This is one aspect of the gift of prophecy, where a believer can predict things. However, this aspect must strictly be done by "being in the Holy Spirit." Otherwise, you could give an erroneous prediction.

[23] Ibid., item 4396.

conjunction with the predictions aspect. But now there aren't any predictions to be given as far as revelation that comes from God is concerned. This is because our present canon of Scripture is completely sufficient for the church dispensation.

So the primary function of the gift of prophecy in the church age is to speak forth what is recorded for us in the Bible. This is the meaning of the "inspired speaking" definition found in Strong's dictionary, which also speaks of a prophet as being a kind of a poet.

7.   Discerning of Spirits.
"Discerning" is *diakrisis* in Greek and means "a judicial estimation."[24] "Spirit" is *pneuma,* meaning "breeze."[25] So this gift is the special ability to determine what kind of spirit is in the vicinity.

8.   Different Kinds of Tongues.
Tongues is *glossa* in Greek and means "a naturally unacquired language."[26] This means it is a known language and not gibberish. So it is the special ability to speak in a known language, but one that has not been learned by the speaker.

One of its purposes is to help communicate with people who do not speak or understand your language when there is no other means available for communicating with them. This

---

[24]   Strong, op. cit., item 1253.

[25]   Ibid., item 4151.

[26]   Ibid., item 1100.

usually happens in a church service and is employed when people are present who do not speak the native language.

However, this gift is becoming less and less necessary as time goes by. This is because knowledge is increasing (Dan. 12:4), including the knowledge of each other's languages. Because of this it is slowly coming to cessation (1 Cor. 13:8c).

The second purpose for tongues is found in 1 Corinthians 14:2. There it says people can speak in tongues while praying, but it also says it is only beneficial for the person doing it (1 Cor. 14:2,4).

A third aspect of tongues is when it is manifested during a church service (I Cor. 14:5). There should always be an interpretation following it (1 Cor. 14:5, 13, 28),[27] and it should be done without any chaos involved (1 Cor. 14:29-33,40).

To summarize, there are three aspects for the gift of tongues. The gift of tongues is for the purpose of communicating with people who do not understand your language, for prayer, and for the edification of others in a church meeting.

9.   Interpretation of Tongues.

"Interpretation" is *hermeneia* in Greek and means "translation."[28] "Tongues," of course, is *glossa,* as mentioned earlier. This, then, is the method the Lord has provided in this day and age for translation work.

---

[27] This is one reason prophecy is preferred over tongues; there might not always be someone present in the congregation with the gift of interpretation of tongues. See 1 Corinthians 14:1, 5, 13, 19.

[28] Strong, op. cit., item 2058.

However, as we have seen, there are two aspects to it. One is so everyone who is present when the gift of tongues is manifested in a church meeting can understand what is being said; the other is the modern day translation of the Scriptures into languages of the world that do not have them.

However, as the gift of tongues becomes less necessary, I feel this gift is becoming more necessary for translation work. There are still many places in the world that need the Word of God translated into their languages, and as knowledge increases (Dan. 12:4), so does translation work.

B. Gifts Found in Romans 12:6–8

The fascinating thing about this list of spiritual gifts is that it has gerunds describing them giving us a hint as to how they are to be manifested.

1. Prophecy.

This prophecy is the same Greek word, (*propheteia*), which was found in 1 Corinthians 12:10. It is listed three times in the major lists because of its importance.

2. Ministry.

Ministry, or "service" in some translations, is *diakonia* in Greek.[29] It means "relief, or to minister." Rick Yohn, in his book *Discover Your Spiritual Gift and Use It,* says the gift of ministry is, "the [special] ability to give assistance or aid in any

---

[29] Strong, op. cit., item 1248.

121

way that brings strength or encouragement to others."[30] So it is the special ability to see a person's spiritual and emotional, needs and to respond to those needs.

3. Teaching.

The verb "teach" here is *didasko* in Greek[31] and means "to impart knowledge." An alternate definition is "causing people to learn."[32] The gerund that follows is *didaskalia*,[33] which means "a teaching," or a doctrine. So the admonition here in Romans 12:7 is to instruct so people will learn doctrine.

4. Exhortation.

The Greek word for "exhortation" is *paraklesis*.[34] It means "comfort; consolation; or, an entreaty." In other words, it is the special ability to urge people toward the things of God in a loving way.

5. Giving.

The Greek word for giving is *metadidomi*,[35] and it means "to give over to." It can also be defined as "the proper use of temporal means in relation to others."[36]

---

[30] Rick Yohn, *Discover Your Spiritual Gift and Use It* (Carol Stream, IL: Tyndale House Publishers, Inc., 1974), 128.

[31] Strong, op. cit., item 1321.

[32] Yohn, op. cit., 76.

[33] Strong, op. cit., item 1319.

[34] Ibid., item 3874.

[35] Ibid., item 3330.

[36] Peter N. Reoch, "Spiritual Gifts in the New Testament," which is section F of point G, of a syllabus for a Christian education course. The

6. Ruling.

The Greek word for ruling is *proistemi,*[37] meaning "to preside over." Rick Yohn says it is "the [special] ability to lead others and manage the affairs of the church."[38] This being the case, a pastor would usually have this gift.

7. Showing Mercy.

Mercy is *eleeo* in Greek[39] and means "to have compassion on." It also is "the [special] ability to work joyfully with those whom the majority ignores."[40]

C. Gifts Found in Ephesians 4:11

1. Apostle.

The Greek word for "apostle" is *apostolos.*[41] It means "one that is sent." This is the term that describes our modern-day missionaries.[42] It is their job to go out and pioneer new work for the Lord.

---

syllabus is titled *Foundations of Christian Education* (Ankeny, Iowa: Faith Baptist Bible College Press, 1977).

[37] Strong, op. cit., item 4291.

[38] Yohn, op. cit., 129.

[39] Strong, op. cit., item 1653.

[40] Yohn, op. cit., 128.

[41] Strong, op. cit., item 652.

[42] Theodore H. Epp, in his book *Gifts of the Spirit* (Lincoln, NB: Back to the Bible Publishing, 1954), agrees with this on page 22.

2. *Prophet.*

The Greek word for prophet is *prophetes*. Just as it was for the gift of prophecy, there are two meanings for *prophetes* in Greek. One is "a foreteller," and the other is "an inspired speaker."[43] However, since it was the job of Old Testament prophets to foretell and there is nothing more to foretell, as far as revelation is concerned (Rev. 22:18), we will have to concede the second meaning is the one valid for the New Testament. This means a prophet is someone known for his or her preaching.

3. Evangelist.

The Greek word for "evangelist" is *euaggelistes* and means "a preacher of the gospel."[44] It is closely related to the Greek word *euaggelizo*[45] which means "to declare good tidings." Therefore, an evangelist is a person with the special ability to present the "good news" of salvation to humankind. The evangelist is usually known as a person who preaches so people will accept Christ as their personal savior.

Even though every believer is admonished to preach the gospel (2 Tim. 4:5; Prov. 11:30; Acts 1:8), it is the evangelist who preaches to a large number of people. So this gift functions outside the local church as well as it does inside. This means when an individual has this spiritual gift, he or she is able to have large meetings to bring many unsaved people to Jesus Christ.

---

[43] Strong, op. cit., item 4396.

[44] Ibid., item 2099.

[45] Ibid., item 2097.

4. Pastor.

The Greek word for "pastor" is *poimen* and means "to shepherd."[46]
In Acts 20:28, these individuals are called "overseers."

Pastors are the leaders of the local congregation and would most likely, then, also have the gift of leadership, or ruling, as described in Romans 12:8.

5. Teacher.

The gift of being a teacher is either when someone is known as being a teacher within the body of Christ, or when someone actually has a teaching position within the local church. It is *didaskalos* in Greek and means "an instructor."[47]

It is possible to have the gift of teaching without the office, because the gift of teaching can be manifested at anytime and at any place in society. However, it is inadvisable to be a teacher within the local church without the gift of teaching. Then you would be teaching in the "self" and not in the Spirit.

It is the same with the gift of being a prophet and also an evangelist. You could be a preacher on a street corner and not preach in a local church.

II. The Two Minor Lists of Spiritual gifts

There are two minor lists of spiritual gifts found in the Bible. They are in 1 Corinthians 12:28 and 1 Corinthians 14:26. They give us two additional spiritual gifts.

---

[46] Strong, op. cit., item 4166.

[47] Ibid., item 1320.

A. 1 Corinthians 12:28

This list of spiritual gifts is an amalgamated list with gifts taken from the three main lists. Its purpose is to show us which gifts are the most important and which are the least. It gives us one of the two new spiritual gifts.

1. Apostles, or apostolos in Greek.
It means "messengers, or ones who are sent." It is the same gift that is found in Ephesians 4:11.

2. Prophets, or prophetes in Greek.
It means "an inspired speaker" and is the same gift that is found in 1 Corinthians 12:10 and Ephesians 4:11.

3. Teachers, or didaskalos in Greek.
It means "instructors" in Greek and is the same gift that is found in Ephesians 4:11, as well as in Romans 12:7.

4. Miracles, or dunamis in Greek.
It means "mighty work for the Lord" and is the same gift that is found in 1 Corinthians 12:10.

5. Healings, or iama in Greek.
It means "cures" and is the same gift that is found in 1 Corinthians 12:9.

6.   Helps, or antilepsis in Greek.

Antilepsis means "relief."[48] It is similar to the gift of ministry found in Romans 12:7, but it is not the same. This gift has more to do with the physical and temporal, whereas the gift of ministry has more to do with the spiritual and psychological aspects of helping someone. Since there is a difference, it is one of the two new spiritual gifts found in the minor lists of spiritual gifts.

7.   Governments, or kubernesis in Greek.

It means "pilotage or directorship,"[49] and is the same as "ruling" in Romans 12:8. This being the case, it is not a new spiritual gift in these minor lists of spiritual gifts.

8.   Tongues, or glossa in Greek.

It means "languages" and is the same gift that is found in 1 Corinthians 12:10.

It will be seen, then, that there is one new spiritual gift, which is helps, in this list of spiritual gifts.

B.   1 Corinthians 14:26

The five entities in this list are emanations from spiritual gifts, so they are not the gifts themselves. They are the results of manifesting the gifts.

---

[48]   Strong, op. cit., 484.

[49]   Ibid., 2941.

127

1. A psalm, or psalmos in Greek.[50]

Psalmos is the musical ability given to people by the Lord. It includes the ability to write music as well as poetry. It has not been mentioned so far as a spiritual gift, and is therefore a new spiritual gift.

2. A teaching, or didache in Greek.[51]

This can also be described as being a doctrine. This being the case, it is the result of the gift of faith, the same as prophesying would be the result of the gift of prophecy. Faith was mentioned while studying the gifts found in 1 Corinthians 12:8–10, so it is not the result of a new gift.

3. A revelation, or apokalupsis in Greek.

It means "to take off the cover, or to disclose,"[52] and is usually labeled a "word of knowledge." But it is not the same thing as the gift of word of knowledge found in 1 Corinthians 12:8.

It is, however, what is necessary for a minister to do his work. So it is not a new gift and only emanates from the gift of ministry.

4. A tongue, or glossa in Greek.

This is the result of the same gift that is found in 1 Corinthians 12:10.

---

[50] Strong, op. cit., item 5568.

[51] Ibid., item 1322.

[52] Ibid., items 601 and 602.

5. An interpretation, or hermeneia in Greek.

As we saw in 1 Corinthians 12:8-10, *hermeneia* means "translation"[53] and is the special ability to translate from one language to another.

Here in 1 Corinthians 14:26 it is the result of the gift found in I Corinthians 12:8-10. It refers to the translation work that is involved when missionaries go out to minister and preach to other cultures. So it is not a new gift, but is an emanation from the gift of interpretation of tongues.

The gift of psalms is an additional spiritual gift in this list that has not been mentioned yet. This being the case, it gives us another new spiritual gift to be added to the collection.

III. The Three Supporting Places Where Spiritual Gifts Are Mentioned in the New Testament

There are three additional places in the New Testament where information is found that supports and gives us advice on how to manifest spiritual gifts. They are 1 Peter 4:11, 2 Corinthians 8:7 and 1 Corinthians 12:4–6.

A. 1 Peter 4:11

First Peter 4:11 gives us two categories of spiritual gifts: speaking and ministry. For instance, the gift of prophecy is a speaking

---

[53] Strong, op. cit., item 2058.

gift, and healing is a ministry gift. Likewise, exhortation is a speaking gift, and showing mercy is a ministry gift.

And the rest of them are just as easily categorized.

B. 2 Corinthians 8:7

Second Corinthians 8:7 tells us how spiritual gifts are to be manifested. And that is with as much faith, utterance, knowledge, diligence, and love for others as possible. In this way, we can "abound" in grace (see also 2 Cor. 9:8).

C. 1 Corinthians 12:4–6

First Corinthians 12:4–6 gives the modal sense in which spiritual gifts are manifested. In other words, the gifts are a part of the indwelling of the Holy Spirit (verse 4), it is the wish of Jesus Christ that spiritual gifts be used to serve and speak to one another (verse 5), and they are a part of God the Father's overall operations of love for humankind (verse 6).

CHAPTER 17

∞

Additional Information about Spiritual Gifts

I.   The Sum Total of All the Gifts

We have seen that there are twenty-one spiritual gifts listed in the three main lists of spiritual gifts. However, prophecy is actually listed three times, because prophecy is what a prophet does. This makes the three entities listed one gift bringing the total to 19 spiritual gifts. Also, teacher is listed twice in these lists, and as a result it brings the total to 18.

We have also seen that two new spiritual gifts are listed in the minor lists. This brings the total of spiritual gifts to twenty.

I have left all five different gifts listed in Ephesians 4:11 intact. The gift of being a teacher is sometimes combined with the gift of being a pastor in Ephesians 4:11, and it is done on the authority of the Grandville-Sharp rule. The Grandville-Sharp rule states that, "when you have two nouns and a 'the' does not appear between them, they are equal or equivalent." For instance, there is a 'the' between apostles, prophets, evangelists and pastors, but not between pastors and teachers.

However, it will be seen that this does not apply to plurals, because the Grandville-Sharp rule is in effect throughout the New Testament for Sadducees and Pharisees, but they are not the same thing. This being the case, pastors and teachers are two different entities and the total for spiritual gifts remains at 20.

II. Some of the Combinations of Spiritual Gifts That Result from Cross-Multiplication

If cross-multiplication were to enter the picture, there would be 400 combinations that could be given to members of the Body of Christ. For example, a person could be an evangelist and have the gift of faith to help with sermon content. And the evangelist could have the gift of prophecy to help in the delivery of the sermons.

Likewise, a pastor could have the gift of showing mercy, as well as the gift of ministry so as to be of help to his or her flock. These would be in addition to the gifts of prophecy, word of wisdom, or word of knowledge to help in sermon delivery.

Out in the world, a layperson could be an executive in a large corporation, be saved by the blood of Jesus Christ, and have the gift of ruling to help be an effective witness to the Lord by doing it in a godly way. A nurse could have the gift of showing mercy, and a doctor the gifts of healing.

III. The Spiritual Gifts Are Very Helpful in Doing Work for
    the Lord

One of the most important aspects of being a Christian is
fulfilling the Great Commission (Matt. 28:19,20). The spiritual
gifts help and aid Christians in doing this by assuring that their
work will be done in God's way.

Conclusion

I wrote this book so that it would be a resource in aiding a person in being "diligent to present [him or herself] approved to God, a worker who does not need to be ashamed" (2 Tim 2:15). The old King James version of the Bible says in 2 Timothy 2:15, "study to shew thyself approved unto God." It is my prayer that this book will be a helpful resource in studying the Word of God, so as to be able "to give a defense to everyone who asks you a reason for the hope that is in you" (1 Pet. 3:15).